Managing Your
MONEY

Personal Finance for Kids

Learn to
EARN, SPEND, SAVE,
and more!

Managing Your MONEY
Personal Finance for Kids

Table of Contents

Money, Money, Money

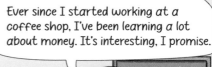

You'll need to learn more about earning money first. You can't manage your money until you know what you're making. Then spending, of course.

I think I know that part pretty well.

And saving— there are tons of ways to save your money.

And then if you make it through all of that, we can talk about credit and investing. I'm still learning about that myself.

How did you learn all of this? I'm impressed.

I had some help. My cousin Hannah runs her own business, so she's an expert at managing money.

Phew, I'm hungry just thinking about all of that. Can I have that money?

Sure. Speaking of credit, you'll need to pay me back for that later. I'm not an ATM!

Thanks! I'll get some snacks. Then you can tell me about credit or whatever.

Ready to start? Let's go!

Earning

I never know how much I'm going to earn. Every paycheck is a complete surprise.

Not for long! We'll figure it out together. Now let's go for a walk. There is a new store downtown I want to show you.

You're already spending that paycheck, huh?

Nice try. Not yet!

Ok, we're here! There's someone I'd like you to meet.

Hi, I'm Hannah.

The famous Hannah! The Budgeting Queen!

That's me!

Hannah had to become an expert in managing money in order to open her store. It's not easy running a business!

And now that I've learned so much about money, I love sharing what I know! I'd be happy to help you out.

3 Careers

So, first things first. Let's talk about jobs. There are many different types of jobs to choose from.

I love my job at the café!

My teacher helped me get my job at the library. But I don't know what else is out there.

Let's look at some examples. You spend a lot of time at work, so it's important to choose a job you think you will enjoy. But that's not the only thing to consider. Some jobs also require more education.

Like college?

Exactly. Some jobs require a college degree. Some even need an advanced degree, like a Master's degree or a Ph.D.

Like teachers, and doctors!

Yup. And some jobs don't require a college degree, but you still need to train and get a certificate.

I know college can be expensive.

Yes, so it's good to make a plan.

Ok, show me those examples you mentioned.

Career Ideas

Fill in the chart below, and include some jobs that you are interested in. You can use job postings to find requirements, descriptions, and salary ranges. You can also look at websites like Glassdoor.com.

Job	Description	Average Salary	Requirements Needed
teacher	Different grades and subjects Besides teaching, also prepare lessons, grade, and meet with students and parents		Master's degree
nurse			
real estate agent			

A salary is the amount of money received in payment for regular work, usually per year.

4 Your Own Plan

✦✦✳✦✦✳✦✦✳✦✦✳✦✦✳✦✦✳✦✦✳✦✦✳✦✦✳✦✦✳✦✦✳✦

Now it's your turn! What job interests you? Use the internet to research the career path you are interested in, or ask someone you know who has this job.

Not sure where to look? In general, government websites such as the website for the Bureau of Labor Statistics are reliable sources of information. You can also look at job resource sites like Glassdoor and Indeed.

What job are you interested in?

Why do you think you would enjoy this job?

What degrees or trainings will you need to complete?

What types of pay and benefits will you receive? Benefits are things given to you by a job in addition to your salary or wage. They can include things like health insurance and retirement plans.

Are there any other jobs that are similar to the one you've chosen? List them here:

What other jobs are you interested in researching further?

Think about subjects in school that you enjoy, or activities that you like doing. For example, if you love science class, maybe you would enjoy being a doctor. If you love art, then maybe you would enjoy working in a museum.

Wages and Salaries

I have a question for you, Sam. How much do you make at the library?

I make $10 an hour.

So you earn an hourly wage. I do too! But did you know that some workers earn a yearly salary?

Does that mean they only get paid once a year?

Luckily, no! They get paid every few weeks just like you do. But when they are hired, their employer tells them how much they will get paid in a year instead of how much they get paid per hour.

Hmm, that sounds a little confusing. It seems hard to compare the amount of money you make from a salaried job with an hourly wage.

Luckily it's pretty easy to figure out! Let's try!

1. a. Eileen earns $25 per hour, and she works 40 hours each week. How much money does she make in a week?

$25 x 40 =

   b. If Eileen works 52 weeks per year, how much will she make in a year?

$1,000 x 52 =

   c. So what is Eileen's salary?

2. Yingxi makes $27 per hour. If she works 40 hours per week, every week, how much will she make in a year?

$27 x   x   =

Remember, there are 52 weeks in a year.

3. a. Aiden earns a salary of $57,200, and he works 52 weeks per year. How much money does he make in a week?

$57,200 ÷ 52 =

   b. If he works 40 hours each week, what is his hourly wage?

$1,100 ÷ 40 =

4. Hillary earns $62,400 in a year. She works 40 hours every week. What is her hourly wage?

$62,400 ÷   ÷   =

This question is just like the others, but in reverse! I'll divide to get the answer.

6 Calculating with Pay Periods

1. Eliza makes $93,600 per year. If her job pays her every two weeks, how much does she make each time she gets paid?

   52 weeks in a year divided by two weeks= _____ weeks

   (This is the number of pay periods per year.)

   $93,600 ÷ _____ = $_____ every two weeks

2. Sera earns $39,000 each year. If she is paid every two weeks, how much does she make each pay period?

3. Richard earns $54,000 each year. If he is paid twice per month, how much does he make each pay period?

   12 months x 2 = _____ pay periods per year

   $54,000 ÷ _____ = $_____ each pay period

Each job can set their own pay periods. Most jobs pay their employees every two weeks (26 paychecks in a year) or twice per month (24 paychecks in a year). But some may pay every week or once a month. You have to ask when you start a new job.

4. Sinclair earns $113,000 per year. If he is paid twice per year, how much does he make each pay period?

5. Maureen gets paid $3,230 twice per month. What is her annual salary?

6. Lin gets paid $500 every other week. What is her annual salary?

7. Thom gets paid $2,700 twice per month. What is his annual salary?

8. Frank gets paid $2,160 every other week. What is his annual salary?

Wages with Tip and Commission

Ok, now I have a question. You earn tips at work, right?

That's correct!

So how do you calculate how much you earn each week?

Great question! I never know exactly how much I'll earn, but I have a pretty good estimate. I know how much I make per hour, so that part is easy. I don't know what my tips will be—that can vary a lot depending on how busy we are and how generous the customers are that day! But I keep track of how much I earn, so I can calculate the average amount. Although the amount I receive varies day to day, knowing the average helps me to have an idea of what to expect.

Oh man. I think I need to see an example.

I earn $15 an hour. That's the minimum wage for all employees in this state, which means that everyone here must earn at least $15 per hour. Last week I made $30 in tips on Monday, $20 on Wednesday, and $40 on Saturday. That adds up to a total of $90 for three shifts. And if I divide $90 by three, then I know that I make an average of $30 in tips each shift.

Ok, that makes sense.

And here's one more thing that can affect your pay check: commissions. When my employees make a sale, I pay them 5% of the sale as a commission. Let's try calculating some examples together.

1. Tory makes $15/hour in a bagel shop and earns an average of $45 in tips per shift. How much will she earn in a week where she works two shifts, and each shift is eight hours?

   Wage: 8 hours x 2 = _____ hours. $15 x _____ hours = $_____

   Tips: $45 x 2 = $_____

   Total: $_____ + $_____ = $_____

2. Sunita makes $10/hour in a restaurant and earns an average of $130 in tips each shift. How much will she earn in a week where she works four shifts, and each shift is seven hours?

   Wage:

   Tips:

   Total:

3. Taylor works in a clothing store. He earns $17 an hour and works 40 hours a week. He earns 5% commission on his sales. How much will he make in a week where he sells $1,200 worth of clothing?

   Wage: $17 x 40 = $_____

   Commission: $1,200 x 5% = $1,200 x 0.05 = $_____

   Total: $_____ + $_____ = $_____

4. Stephanie earns $13 an hour at a shoe store and works 35 hours a week. She makes 7% commission on each pair of shoes she sells. How much does she make in a week where she sells $2,000 worth of shoes?

   Wage:

   Commission:

   Total:

Each state sets their own minimum wage, so the minimum wage varies depending on where you live. And keep in mind: some employees can be paid less than minimum wage—as long as they are receiving tips! For example, if the minimum wage is $15 per hour in your state, you could be paid $10 an hour from your employer. As long as you receive at least $5 in tips each hour, you will still get $15 an hour, which is why this is allowed. This is very common in restaurants.

Calculating Wages

✦✦✳✦✦✦✦✳✦✦✦✦✳✦✦✦✦✦✳✦✦✦✦✳✦✦✦✳✦✦✦✳✦

1. Earnest is paid $9.50 an hour at a restaurant. This week, he works an 8-hour shift, a 7-hour shift, and two 7.5-hour shifts. He earns the following in tips: $65, $54, $85, and $87.

   a. How much does he earn this week?

   Wage: $9.50 × _____ + $9.50 × _____ + $9.50 × _____ + $9.50 × _____ = $_____

   Tips: $_____ + $_____ + $_____ + $_____ = $_____

   Total: $_____ + $_____ = $_____

   b. What does he average in tips per shift?

   $_____ ÷ 4 shifts = $_____

2. Samantha is paid $8.75 an hour at a restaurant. In one week, she works two 9-hour shifts, a 7-hour shift, and two 8.5-hour shifts. She earns the following in tips: $94, $110, $63, $44, and $77.

   a. How much does she earn this week?

   Wage:

   Tips:

   Total:

   b. What does she average in tips per shift?

3. Ellie is paid $9.85 an hour at a café. In one week, she works two 8-hour shifts and two 8.5-hour shifts. She earns the following in tips: $64, $70, $83, and $71.

  a. How much does she earn this week?

  Wage:

  Tips:

  Total:

  b. What does she average in tips per shift?

4. Tim is paid $10.50 an hour at a coffee shop. In one week, he works two 8-hour shifts, a 7.5-hour shift, and two 6.5-hour shifts. He earns the following in tips: $67, $84, $89, $71, and $82.

  a. How much does he earn this week?

  Wage:

  Tips:

  Total:

  b. What does he average in tips per shift?

9 Income Tax

Ok, here's a question—why do I always get less money than I think I will? When I calculate how much I make, I get one number. But when the paycheck comes, it's a completely different number. And it's way lower!

Yes! That's because of taxes. And other stuff . . . Honestly, this gets pretty complicated, so I'm going to need Hannah to explain.

Let's talk about taxes first. Everyone pays income taxes to the federal government, and in most states, you are also taxed on your income. Some places even have a local tax. Your taxes are a percentage of your income, and they are based on the amount you earn in a year. It's a little complicated to calculate. We'll look at some examples together so that you can get a sense of how it works.

Ugh, why do I even have to pay taxes? It's so unfair.

Well, our government needs the money to pay its employees and to build things for the public like schools and roads. But no one enjoys seeing that money come out of their paycheck! The important thing is to remember that these taxes exist, and to keep them in mind when you're planning.

So how do you know how much to pay?

Luckily your employer will do the math for you! And it's tricky. You pay a percentage that increases as you make more money.

I have a question. I hear everyone complain about paying taxes in April. But it seems like we pay taxes all year round!

Great point. If you are earning money, you have to file taxes every year in April. That means filling out paperwork, and it's not fun! But if your job has been deducting taxes from your paycheck all year, then you'll probably find that you don't owe any money—or at least not much. It's even possible that you may have overpaid, and you might get a refund check!

Yes please!

1. Imagine you live in Seattle. You earn $40,000 a year and you pay federal taxes only. Let's see how much you would earn in a two-week period. Round your answer to two decimal places.

 Lucky for us, there is no state tax in Washington! So we only have to worry about federal tax in this problem.

$40,000 ÷ 26 (since there are 52 weeks in a year, there are 26 two-week periods in a year)

= $_____ per week.

Federal tax = You will be taxed on ten percent of the first $11,000 you earn, and twelve percent on the rest of your income. Determine:

A. 10% of $11, 000 ($_____);

B. 12% of the difference between $40,000 and $11,000.

$40,000 − $11,000 = $_____. Multiply by 0.12 to get $_____.

Add **A** + **B** to get your federal taxes for the year: $_____

Divide by 26 to get the amount for a two week period: $_____

Subtract it from the total you earn in a two week period: $_____

Phew! I told you it was tricky. Luckily most jobs do this math for you. You only need to figure this out if you are self-employed and don't have a boss!

10 Social Security

There's something else you might have noticed on your paycheck. Social Security! It's also referred to as FICA, or Federal Insurance Contributions Act.

Yes, I've seen that before. What is it, exactly? More taxes?

Well, it might feel like a tax in the sense that it comes out of your paycheck and helps contribute to something that benefits everyone. But it's different from income tax.

That's right! Social Security is a program that collects payments from people who are currently working. Then when you are older, you receive payments from Social Security that help you pay for things after you retire.

How old do you have to be to get Social Security payments?

Right now the earliest age is 62. So you have a long ways to go! Although, people with disabilities who are over 18 can receive Social Security benefits if they are not able to work.

Should we look at some examples?

1. Cynthia earns $52,000 per year. Employees pay 6.2% of their income to Social Security. How much does Cynthia pay for Social Security in a two-week period? (Remember that there are 52 weeks in year.)

   $52,000 ÷ (52 ÷ 2) = $52,000 ÷ _____ = $_____

   $_____ x 6.2% = $_____ x 0.062 = $_____

Everyone pays 6.2% of their income to Social Security unless they earn more than the limit. In 2023, that amount is $160,200. If you earn more than that, you are still only paying 6.2% of $160,200. So if you earn $200,000, you are only paying 6.2% of $160,200, and not 6.2% of $200,000.

2. Dante earns $135,200 per year. How much does he pay for Social Security in a two-week period?

3. Fatima earns $78,000 per year. How much does she pay for Social Security in a month?

4. Alicia earns $35 per hour. If she works 40 hours per week, how much does she pay for Social Security in a week?

5. Santos earns $40 per hour and works 35 hours per week. How much does he pay for Social Security in a two-week period?

Health Insurance

Sam and Maya, I don't suppose you get any other employee benefits, do you?

I get a free coffee or tea each shift!

I get to borrow books for free . . . but then again, I guess everyone who goes to the library gets that benefit.

Well, those are pretty good perks, I must admit! But I mean employee benefits. That includes health insurance, retirement benefits, paid time off, or commuter benefits.

Nope! I don't get anything like that.

Me either.

They're more common for full-time jobs. Part-time employees don't always get these benefits. But it's worth talking about because they can affect your paycheck.

How does it affect your paycheck?

For example, when you have health insurance through your job, your employer pays for some of the cost. But you pay for some too, and it comes out of your paycheck. It gets taken out before your taxes are calculated. So you don't pay taxes on that part of your income.

Hmm. I think I might need to see some examples before I understand.

1. Regina earns $112,800 per year. She gets paid twice per month. She pays $250 per month for health insurance, which is split between the two paychecks she gets each month.

   a. How much does she earn before taxes on each paycheck?

   $112,800 ÷ (12 x 2) = $112,800 ÷ 24 = $_____ per paycheck

   b. How much does she earn after health insurance is subtracted?

   $250 ÷ 2 = $_____ health insurance deducted per pay check

   $_____ − $_____ = $_____

   > So Regina pays taxes on $__4,575__ instead of on $__4,700__.

2. Chris earns $74,400 per year. He gets paid twice per month. He pays $345 per month for health insurance, which is split between the two paychecks he gets each month.

   a. How much does he earn before taxes on each paycheck?

   b. How much does he earn after health insurance is subtracted?

3. Ayelet earns $51,480 per year. She gets paid every two weeks. She pays $240 per month for health insurance, which comes out of the first paycheck for each month.

   a. How much does she earn before taxes on the first paycheck of each month?

   b. How much does she earn after health insurance is subtracted?

Retirement Accounts

 So, we've already discussed health insurance. Retirement accounts work similarly. Your employer will set up a retirement account for you where you can save money for your retirement. Your employer may contribute some money to this account, but mostly it is a place for you to put your savings. That money comes out of your paycheck, and it also comes out before taxes.

Why is it called a retirement account?

 Because the money you put in there should be saved until you retire. If you withdraw your money early, you will have to pay tax plus a penalty. So it's best to leave it there.

What about commuter benefits?

 Great question. Some jobs allow you to put aside the money you spend commuting to work into a separate account. Then you can use it to buy bus tickets or whatever else you need. And—you guessed it—that money is taken out before taxes too. So it's another way to reduce the amount of income tax you have to pay.

And what about this "paid time off?"

 That means you still get paid when you go on vacation. Most full-time employees get a certain amount of vacation days each year, and sick days too. That way when you need to take time off, your paycheck stays the same. You won't earn less than usual, even though you worked less.

Sign me up for that one!

1. Francis earns $67,200 per year. She gets paid twice per month. She puts $250 into her retirement account each month, which is split between the two paychecks she gets each month.

   a. How much does she earn before taxes on each paycheck?

   $67,200 ÷ (12 x 2) = $67,200 ÷ 24 = $_____ per paycheck

   b. How much does she earn after her retirement contribution is subtracted?

   $250 ÷ 2 = $_____ retirement contribution per paycheck

   $_____ − $_____ = $_____

   > I've got this one. Francis pays taxes on $_____ instead of on $_____!

2. Mike earns $55,200 per year. He gets paid twice per month. He puts 7% of his income into his retirement account.

   a. How much does he earn before taxes on each paycheck?

   b. How much does he earn after his retirement contribution is subtracted?

3. Tom earns $75,400 per year. He gets paid every two weeks. He puts $400 each month into his retirement account, which comes out of the first paycheck for each month.

   a. How much does he earn before taxes on the first paycheck of each month?

   b. How much does he earn after subtracting his retirement contribution?

Gross Income and Net Income

Ok, guys! We've talked about all of the things that get deducted from your paycheck separately. Now I want to put it all together. It's time to talk about gross income and net income.

Excuse you! My income is not gross!

Sam! Gross has more than one meaning!

Your gross income is the amount you make before taxes, Social Security, health insurance, retirement savings . . . all that good stuff. It's the big number you see before all of those things get subtracted.

So net income is the amount you actually get?

Exactly. Your net income is the income you receive once everything has been deducted.

And those numbers can be pretty different. I'm always surprised by how big the difference can be.

Yup! And it's why you should always budget your spending using your net income—we'll discuss that more later.

First we'll look at some examples, right?

You know it!

1. Myra earns $65,000 per year. She is paid every two weeks, and puts 3% of each paycheck into her retirement account. She lives in Los Angeles and pays state and federal taxes. Search online for a California income tax calculator, and use that to calculate her taxes and what is left over afterwards. Round to the nearest two decimal places.

> Go online and search for the keywords "income tax calculator California." That will calculate taxes, including Social Security. Then you can subtract other benefits (like her retirement contribution) yourself.

2. If Myra made $75,000 per year, with no other change, what would her net income be? How much greater would it be than her income in #1? Round to the nearest two decimal places.

14 More Practice with Net Income

+ + + ✳ + + + ✳ + + + + ✳ + + + ✳ + + + ✳ + + + ✳ + + + ✳ + + + ✳

Use an online calculator to solve the following activities.

1. Tenzin earns $102,000. He lives in Florida, where there is no state income tax. He is paid bi-monthly, and $70 is deducted from each paycheck for health insurance. He sets aside $180 per month for commuting, which is split equally between both paychecks. He pays 8% of his income into a retirement account. He pays 6.2% into Social Security. What does his net paycheck look like?

Gross pay:

Gross pay per paycheck:

Paycheck minus commuting:

Paycheck minus Social Security, retirement savings, and federal tax
(use online calculator for this step):

Net paycheck:

> What taxes do you have to pay in your hometown?
> Ask an adult or use the internet to research.

2. Grecia earns $89,960. She lives in Denver, Colorado and pays local, state, and federal income taxes. She is paid every other week, and $460 is deducted from each paycheck for health insurance. She pays 6% of her income into a retirement account. She pays 6.2% into Social Security. What does her net paycheck look like?

Gross pay:

Gross pay per paycheck:

Paycheck minus health insurance:

Paycheck minus Social Security, retirement savings, and taxes
(use online calculator for this step):

Net paycheck:

That was a lot of math. I'm ready to move on to the fun part—Spending!

15 Earning Review

✦+✦+✱+✦+✦+✱+✦+✦+✱+✦+✦+✱+✦+✦+✱+✦+✦+✱+✦+✦+✱

We learned a lot in this chapter! Let's review:

★ How to choose a job

★ The difference between hourly and salaried jobs

★ Different pay periods

★ Tips and commissions

★ Income tax

★ Social Security

★ Health insurance contributions

★ Retirement account contributions

★ Other paycheck deductions

★ Calculating gross and net pay

And best of all—how to get paid for not working!
I need to figure out that whole paid time off thing.

Spending

I told you guys already— I KNOW how to spend money. In fact, I'll teach you.

Lesson One: If it's under $10, it's basically free.

Lesson 2: If it's on sale, you're practically losing money if you don't buy it.

SALE

And Lesson 3: If you're not sure about something, just buy it! You can always return it later.

SALE

Oh boy we're really starting from square one, aren't we?

I'm afraid so.

Let's face it. I'm better at spending money than you.

Technically, you're good at spending money. But you're not spending money wisely.

I can see why your money disappears so quickly.

Ok, so what am I doing wrong?

You need a budget!

You need to learn the difference between needs and wants.

You need to track your spending. I bet you don't even realize how much you spend in a month.

And you need to learn to resist the urge to buy everything that catches your eye.

Sounds boring. But fine. I'm listening.

And I bet you forget to return the things you don't like sometimes. Am I right?

Those cheap purchases add up in a hurry.

Ok, so we've got to talk about being a smart shopper.

Well, sometimes . . .

That means resisting marketing techniques designed to make you spend more money.

It also means spending an amount of money that matches your income.

And if I do that, what do I get out of it?

You get the confidence in knowing that you have enough money for everything you need—because you haven't overspent on unnecessary things.

Well, I guess this won't be as much fun as I imagined. But that sounds worth it.

17 Advertising Tricks

Let's talk about some common advertising tricks.

I've got one! Peer pressure.

Great example! Peer pressure is when you feel like you need to do something in order to fit in with what everyone else is doing. Advertisements sometimes use this to get consumers to buy their products. For instance an ad might say, "Don't miss out on the hot new toy that everyone is playing with!"

Or what about if you notice all your friends have the same sneakers and you don't? And then you feel like you need to wear them too?

That's also a form of peer pressure.

Ok, what else?

Another trick advertisers use is that they make you feel like you need to buy something urgently.

"This deal won't last!"

"Hurry! These won't be available for long!"

 Exactly! They play with your emotions and make you afraid to miss out. If you took the time to think about it, you might realize you really don't need it at all. But they want you to not think too hard—just buy!

Ooh, like when something is limited edition! Those always sell out so quickly.

I want to talk about discounts next.

 Be our guest!

Just because something is on sale doesn't mean you're getting a good deal! Let's say a shirt is priced at $50 and reduced to $45. The shirt is on sale, but it's not cheap!

 Absolutely. And you have to remember that companies know that customers love getting a deal. So sometimes they will set their prices high on purpose, knowing that they will offer a discount anyway. That way they get the amount they really want, and customers feel like they got a deal.

But that's cheating!

 It's not cheating—but it can influence shoppers' decisions. So now you have some ideas for what to look out for the next time you go shopping.

18 Advertising and Peer Pressure

+ ✦ + ✦ + ✳ + + ✦ + + ✳ + ✦ + ✳ + + ✦ + + ✦ + + ✳ + ✦ + ✳ + + ✦ + + ✦ + ✳

It's time to think about what effect advertising has on you. Use the questions below to help you reflect on how advertisers try to influence you into purchasing things.

Where do you see ads? (TV, magazines, social media, billboards, etc). What types of things do you

see advertisements for?

Choose one type of trick advertisers use, and give an example of an ad that you have seen that

uses this technique. Did you think this ad was persuasive? Why or why not?

Have you ever bought something, or asked your parents to buy something, after feeling peer pressure? What was it? How did you feel after you bought it?

What can you do to avoid being tricked by advertising?

Needs and Wants

I can't believe I let you talk me out of buying those pants. They were so cool! I need them.

 Well, you don't NEED them.

 You WANT them. And that's fine. Sometimes we can buy ourselves the things we want. But first we need to buy the things that we need.

What if I said that I want to wear them to a party next week? Does that make it a 'need'?

 Nope, still a 'want'! Think about it. If you didn't buy those pants, then what?

I wear my old stupid pants that I hate. And everyone makes fun of me.

 You have so much cool clothing! I promise no one would care.

 See? You'd be fine. You might enjoy wearing new pants if you had them, but if you don't buy them nothing bad will happen. You'll just wear something you already own.

I guess. Then what would you consider a 'need'?

Luckily, most of your needs are paid for by your parents. For me, the most essential things I need are a place to live, food to eat, and health care. Some clothing items are things I need—for example a winter coat, so I don't get cold on my way to work—but most aren't strictly necessary.

Sam, I have to point out that this whole journey of financial education started when you asked me to borrow money to buy a snack.

True. When I got a job, my parents told me that I'm responsible for paying for my own food when I eat out with friends. And I'm not great at budgeting, so sometimes I run out and have to borrow money from my friends until my next paycheck comes.

So it sounds like that's something you need. You don't want to go to basketball practice feeling hungry. But the pants on the other hand . . .

I guess I could live without them.

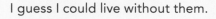

The thing is, buying things you want isn't always bad! Sometimes it's ok to buy a pair of pants you really want! That's one of the perks of having a job in the first place.

The catch is that you can't buy EVERYTHING you want. And you have to make sure you prioritize the things you need first.

20 Sorting Needs and Wants

What are some things in your life that you could not live without? Think about shelter, food, health, and transportation. List the most important things here.

Share your list with your family and ask them if you missed any other essential expenses. List any additional expenses here.

What are some non-essential things your family spends money on? Consider entertainment, fashion, travel.

Do you ever receive money of your own, as a gift, an allowance, or for doing work or chores?

If so, what things do you spend it on? Are these things you need, or things you want?

If you wanted to save some money, what things could you stop spending money on? What things could you not go without?

21 Ways to Pay

 Sam and Maya, how do you usually pay for things?

Is this a trick question? I use money, of course!

 No, no, I mean what form of payment do you use—cash, credit, or debit?

I use cash sometimes, but mostly I use my debit card. It's so much easier!

I use a card. But how do I know if it's debit or credit?

 A debit card is linked to your bank account. When you use it to pay for something, it deducts that money from your account.

And credit cards are like borrowing, right?

 That's right. When you use a credit card, the money doesn't get taken out of your bank account right away. You get a bill at the end of the month with your total spending on it. Then you pay that bill. And there is another difference—usually when you use a debit card, you have to enter a four-digit code, called a PIN.

And a debit card is also what you use to get cash from an ATM, right? That's what I use.

 That's right!

Then this is definitely a debit card.

1. Which payment methods have you used before? Describe the experience of paying this way.

2. What are some pros and cons of each payment method?

Payment Method	Pro	Con
Cash		
Debit		
Credit		

Digital Payments

 Sam, you still owe me that money, remember?

Oh yeah! I just got paid, but I haven't gotten a chance to go to an ATM yet.

 Do either of you ever use any apps to pay for things?

 I do! No need to go to an ATM, Sam!

Really? What apps can you use?

 Venmo is a popular one for sending money to your friends. It takes money directly from your bank account and sends it to them. Paypal works the same way. There is also Zelle, Google Pay, Apple Pay, and many more! Some of them can also be linked to debit or credit cards, which allows you to use them at stores.

 They're so convenient! I love not having to use cash.

 They're convenient, but be careful! First of all, it's easy to lose track of your spending when it all happens at the click of a button. And then there are scams . . .

Scams?! Yikes.

 Just make sure that if you get an unexpected request from a friend, you call them to confirm it's really them. And if anyone offers you money—a reward from a contest you didn't enter, for example—don't respond. They want your information and they're hoping to trick you into sending them money.

1. Have you ever used any of these apps to pay for something? Was it more convenient than using cash?

2. What situations are digital payments helpful in?

3. What are some dangers in using digital payments?

4. What guidelines can you use to make sure you are using these apps responsibly?

23 Checks and Money Orders

There are two last forms of payment we should talk about: checks and money orders.

I know what checks are! I've seen my parents write them out.

And my bank gave me a book of checks when I opened an account. But I've never used any.

Checks aren't used as frequently now that we have so many ways to transfer money digitally. But it's great that you have some—they can come in handy sometimes!

So if I want to use one, I just fill it out and give it to someone? And then what?

Then they take it to a bank or ATM and deposit it. Once they do, the money is transferred from your account to theirs. Sometimes you can also deposit checks from home by using an app.

But what if there isn't enough money in your account? You could write any number you want.

If there isn't enough money, the check 'bounces.' That means it can't go through, and both you and the other person will get charged a fee by your banks. You'll both lose money and they'll be very frustrated with you! So make sure you have enough money in your account.

Ok, so then what's a money order?

A money order is sort of like a check that has been guaranteed by a bank or government. You can get one at a bank, or at the post office. They will make it out to the person you are paying and pull the funds out of your account when they create the money order. When you give someone a money order, they know for sure that they can deposit it without it bouncing.

Practice filling out these checks.

1. Make out a check for $50 to a friend.

DATE _____

PAY TO THE
ORDER OF ___friend's name:_____ $ [50.00]

___fifty dollars and 00/00_____ DOLLARS

MEMO ___optional note_____   ___your signature:_____

2. Write a check of $25 to a family member.

DATE _____

PAY TO THE
ORDER OF _____ $ [   ]

_____ DOLLARS

MEMO _____   _____

Tracking Expenses

If you're trying to get serious about your finances, tracking your expenses is an important first step. You might think you know how much you normally spend, but if you aren't keeping track carefully, the real number may be very different from your estimate! Use this page to track your family's expenses for the next week. Ask your family to help you record everything your family spends money on—at the grocery store or in restaurants, on gas, school supplies, pet food, and more.

Date	Description	Price

Which of the following categories did your family spend the most on: food, entertainment, retail, health? Which did you spend the least on?

Which of these expenses was the most surprising to you? Why?

Do you think this week was a typical week for your family in terms of spending? Why or why not?

If you were creating a budget for your family, what would you prioritize spending on?

We've talked about budgets a lot—but how do I make one?

 I'm glad you asked! First write your income on the top.

 Well, it varies a little each month. But usually I get about $200.

 Great! Now for your expenses. Typically, when you make a budget, you start with your fixed expenses, or the necessities that you have to pay for each month. That includes things like rent, insurance, and transit. Since your family takes care of those things, you don't need to include them in your budget.

Phew!!   What about subscriptions?

 Great point, Maya. Sam, do you have any subscriptions that you pay for? Maybe a streaming site like Netflix, a magazine, or even a newsletter that you subscribe to?

 My parents pay for most of those things. But I do pay for my own Spotify account. I get charged for it every month.

 Ok, so let's record that. Then we'll decide on some categories for the rest of your spending.

Food!   Entertainment!

Transit!   Clothing!

Ok, and I've got two more. Miscellaneous expenses—and savings.

So now what? How much do we allot to each category?

 First we start with what Sam earns, then we subtract his fixed expenses. The remainder gets split up between all of the categories we just listed. We'll use the expenses he's been tracking as a guide.

Sam's Budget

Estimated Monthly Income: $200

Subscriptions: $10
This covers the music Sam streams every month.

Food: $60
This is the money Sam spends on after school snacks or meals he has with his friends.

Entertainment: $30
This covers Sam's expenses when he goes to the movies, or if he decides to buy tickets to a concert or show.

Transit: $20
Sam takes the bus into town to hang out with his friends.

Clothing: $40
Sam's parents pay for the essentials, but this goes towards extra items he wants.

Miscellaneous: $15
Putting some money in a miscellaneous category allows Sam to spend a little extra money in one category without going over budget. For example, if he spends $55 on clothing, but sticks to his budget in every other category, then he'll still be ok. The miscellaneous category is also helpful in case he has to pay for something that he forgot to budget for.

Savings: $25
Sam is saving a little bit of money each month for the future.

Making a Budget

Now we're going to practice creating some budgets. Keep in mind that there are many possible ways someone could choose to budget their money in these scenarios, so there are many correct answers.

1. Julia earns about $250 each month working at a restaurant after school. She lives with her family, so she is not responsible for paying for housing or groceries. However, she spends about $60 on gas to drive herself to school and extracurricular activities. She goes out to eat with her friends every Friday, and typically spends about $35. She also loves going to concerts. Use the chart below to organize her spending. You can enter your own categories at the bottom.

Monthly Income: $250

Expenses:

Transportation	
Entertainment	
Food	
Savings	

Why did you choose to distribute her money in this way? Explain why you assigned the amounts that you did.

2. Eric earns about $200 each month babysitting. His parents cover his essential needs, but he pays for his own expenses when he hangs out with his friends. He goes to the movies with his friends at least once a month, and he buys coffee and a snack at least once a week. He is also saving up to buy a pair of sneakers that cost $200. Use the chart below to create a budget for Eric.

Monthly Income: $200

Expenses:

Food	
Entertainment	
Clothing	
Savings	

Why did you choose to distribute his money in this way? Explain why you assigned the amounts that you did.

27 Your Budget

Now it's time to create your own budget. If you receive any money from your parents or from a job, use your own information and create a budget that will work for you right now! Otherwise, use this scenario: Imagine you are a high school student living with your parents. You earn about $200 per month working in a book store on the weekends. You are responsible for paying for things your parents don't consider essential, including fast food and other treats that you eat after school, and clothing that you don't 'need.' You are hoping to go to a concert in a few months with your friends, and the tickets cost $60.

1. What categories are most important to you?

2. Do you have any recurring charges that you need to pay for?

3. Use the chart below to create a budget.

Monthly Income:

Expenses:

4. Do you think this budget will be easy to stick to? Why or why not?

5. Are there any categories that you are worried you might overspend in? Why?

6. If you stick to this budget, how many months will it take you to save up for the concert tickets?

28 Sales Tax

Well, I've tried sticking to my budget and I've noticed a problem. Sometimes I think I'm spending a certain amount of money, like $15. But when I go to pay for it, it's actually a little bit more. Why is that? Are they scamming me?

That's sales tax. Our state adds an 7% tax on to most items that you buy in the store.

More tax? I thought they took that out of our paychecks already!

That's income tax. Sales tax is collected when you spend money in a store. The store collects the money, and then they pay it to the government.

You said "our state." Does that mean that not every state has sales tax?

That's right. Most do, but there are a few that don't. And the percent varies from state to state.

So how do you know how much you're spending?

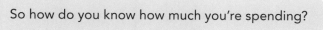

Now that you know it's 7%, you can estimate in your head!

✦✦✦

1. Lisa wants to buy a $20 shirt, a $15 pair of sunglasses, and a $2 pack of gum. Sales tax is 3%. How much will her total be?

   Total without sales tax: $20 + $15 + $2 = $37

   Sales tax: $37 x 3% = $37 x 0.03 = $1.11

   Total with sales tax: $37 + $1.11 = $_____

2. Ben buys three books. One costs $10, one is $12, and one is $18. Sales tax is 6%. What is his total?

   Total without sales tax:

   Sales tax:

   Total with sales tax:

3. Zoe is buying three cases of cat food, which are $30 each. If sales tax is 4.5%, what is her total?

   Total without sales tax:

   Sales tax:

   Total with sales tax:

4. Rocki wants to buy a new case for her phone for $27.60. If sales tax is 7.5%, how much will she spend?

   Total without sales tax:

   Sales tax:

   Total with sales tax:

29 Here's a Tip

I had a difficult day at work today.

I'm sorry to hear that. What went wrong?

There were a lot of demanding customers. So many complaints. And then we barely even got any tips!

Ugh, that is the worst! Sometimes people just don't realize how important tips are to employees.

Can I be honest? Sometimes I'm not sure if I'm tipping well or not. It gets confusing!

It can be a little confusing! Especially because tipping is a custom, and it is different in so many places. In some countries, like Japan, people don't tip at all. In many European countries, people leave small tips. But in the United States, tipping is an important part of an employee's compensation.

Basically, in the United States you should always tip in a restaurant or café. You also tip hairdressers, cab drivers, and delivery people. Oh, and if you get a manicure you have to tip also! You never need to tip in a store, even when an employee helps you find something. But otherwise, you are usually expected to tip anyone whose job involves serving you in some way.

Ok, I think I've got all that. But how much do you tip? Is it 20%?

20% is a standard tip for good service. When in doubt, leave 20%. It's also a nice round number that is pretty easy to calculate in your head.

But here's the thing . . . do I really have to? What happens if I don't?

 Then the employees who help you don't make as much money. We count on those tips, Sam! You need to factor them in when you are budgeting how much you will spend at a restaurant. You should leave a 20% tip.

Ok, ok! I get it now.

Calculate the appropriate tip and total for each bill.

1. Restaurant $60
   Tip: $60 x 20% = $60 x 0.2 = $_____
   Total: $60 + $_____ = $_____

2. Hair salon $55
   Tip:
   Total:

3. Taxi $25
   Tip:
   Total:

4. Café $27
   Tip:
   Total:

5. Restaurant $44
   Tip:
   Total:

6. Nail salon $32
   Tip:
   Total:

7. Food delivery $18
   Tip:
   Total:

 Ok, let's go shopping together.

I thought you'd never ask!   Shopping for what?

 Let's look for a new backpack. I've narrowed it down to 3 options.

Option	Size	Pockets	Additional Features	Price
A	Holds notebooks, textbooks, folders, and pens and pencils. Does not fit a laptop.	Has one main pocket and one pocket for small items.	None.	$30
B	Fits a laptop in addition to all other school supplies.	Has one large space for books, a space for a laptop, and several small pockets.	Adjustable straps for better back support.	$65
C	Fits notebooks, folders, pens and pencils. Does not fit laptop or textbook.	Has many different sized pockets.	Brand name, cool design, and there is a pair of matching sneakers also available for purchase.	$90

Ooh, which one should we buy?!?

 A is the most affordable.

It's also the most basic. It doesn't even hold a laptop! I like C.

 C doesn't hold a laptop either! You just like it because it looks cool.

And it's high quality.

 What makes you say it's high quality?

Well, I know the brand. It's expensive, but it's worth it.

 Just because something is expensive doesn't mean it's high quality! It doesn't hold textbooks either! It's not much of a backpack.

 Many people assume that expensive items are better. But which of these are the most practical?

B holds it all.

 Right. So if you were willing to splurge, B makes the most sense.

 And if you couldn't spend $65 on a backpack and were willing to carry your laptop separately—

Then A makes the most sense.

 So what have we learned from this?

Ugh! I guess it's to think about what we need the most from a product. And to not assume that the cool, expensive one is better.

 That's right.

Comparison Shopping

Now it's your turn to try comparison shopping. Imagine that you are buying a new phone. Find three options, and use the chart below to record some research about each option.

Option	Price	Storage	Speed	Additional Features

Which of these options would you purchase? Why?

Is there another option that you might also consider? Why or why not?

And now, think of something you want to buy and research three options. Create your own categories to evaluate with.

Option			

Which of these would you buy? Why?

Which of these would you definitely not buy? Why?

I like to read customer reviews online before I buy something. Not all reviews are helpful, but sometimes people make an interesting observation that I hadn't considered.

32 Spending Review

We learned a lot in this chapter! Let's review:

★ **Common advertising tricks**

★ **How to resist peer pressure**

★ **The difference between needs and wants**

★ **How to use cash, credit, and debit**

★ **What digital payments are**

★ **The difference between checks and money orders**

★ **How to track expenses and create a realistic budget**

★ **How to calculate sales tax**

★ **How to tip**

We've SPENT a lot of time on this topic! But I think it's worth it.

Saving

That jacket is so cool. I've been looking at it in the window every time I walk past.

Have you tried it on?

No, I don't want to be tempted to buy it. I'm trying to save my money.

Ugh, whatever! I understand now why you shouldn't overspend—but I don't see why saving is such a big deal. It's your money!

Yeah, but I want to be sure I have money for the future. I save a little bit each month, and I've been watching my money grow.

And what will you do with it in the future, Ms. Moneybags?

I'm not sure! Maybe I'll have a big purchase I want to make one day, and I'll need to have some funds saved up to do it.

Or maybe I'll save it until I'm older. I want to travel the world one day!

But in the meantime, it just makes me feel good knowing that I have money saved for the future.

I think that's great, Maya! Saving is so important. The sooner you get in the habit, the better.

What about you, Sam? Now that you're a budgeting expert, are you saving money each month?

Well . . . . sort of. I definitely thought about saving money last month. And I didn't overspend! But I didn't have much left over at the end of the month.

That's a good start! You've come a long way already.

But you should try saving some money each month, even if it's just a little.

I'll give it a shot. Right after I----

No excuses, Sam! I know you can do this.

Ok, ok, fine! I'll try saving $20 each month and see how it goes.

Your future self thanks you!

I mentioned that I have been saving money, but I don't think I'm really doing it the best way. When I get paid, all the money goes into my bank account. And then it's all in one place, and it's a little hard to keep track.

That's what savings accounts are for! Your checking account is great for holding the money you need on a day-to-day basis, but it's not the best place to keep your savings. Setting your savings aside in a separate account will make it easier to keep track of what you're saving. And most importantly, it will help you to earn interest.

But that's where I keep getting stuck. I know that there are different types of accounts, and I just don't know what's right for me.

There are so many types! Let's start with the basics. First, there are regular savings accounts that you can get at your bank—the same place you have your checking account.

That sounds convenient!

It is convenient! But here are the things to look out for: how high the interest rate is, and what type of fees they charge.

I want the interest rate to be as high as possible, right? Because that's how you make more money?

That's right! And of course, you need to make sure the fees aren't too high.

Wait a minute—they charge you money to have a savings account?

Some accounts have a monthly charge. And depending on how high it is, it might cancel out any interest you earn. So you need to know what fees they charge.

What other type of accounts are there?

 Money Market accounts allow you to put away your savings and earn interest. But you can still access your funds with a debit card or a check.

Is there a catch?

 As with traditional savings accounts, you'll have to check their fees and make sure it's worth it for you.

I've also heard of another kind—CDs? What is that?

 Certificates of deposit are accounts where you leave your money for a set amount of time. You'll earn interest on the money you put in, but you can't withdraw your money early or else you'll be charged.

You've also mentioned retirement accounts. How do those work?

 When you work full-time, your job will likely provide a type of account called a 401k. You can make tax-free deposits, and sometimes your employer will contribute to it too. But until then, there is another type of account that you can set up with help from your parents. An IRA is an individual retirement account where you can put away money for retirement. You won't be taxed on the interest that you earn. But you will be charged if you withdraw your money early.

Usually I'm the responsible one, but I don't think I'm ready to start saving for retirement just yet. I want to be able to access my money.

 It's never too early to start saving for retirement! That said, if you care about being able to access your savings, then you should make sure to choose an account that won't penalize you for withdrawing your funds too soon.

Do you have a savings account? If so, what kind? If not, which kind do you think would be best for you?

35 Interest

So here is something I'm INTERESTed in . . . how exactly does your savings account grow?

Great question, Sam! Let's talk about interest. There are two types of interest—simple interest and compound interest. Simple interest is when interest is calculated based on the principal amount—the amount you started with. Compound interest is calculated on the principal as well as interest earned in previous years.

Let's keep it simple for now, please.

Your wish is my command!

Here's a formula for calculating simple interest:
Interest = Principal x Rate x Time

Calculate the following:

1. How much interest will you earn on $1,000 at 5% interest for a year?

$1,000 x 5% =

2. How much interest will you earn on $400 at 8% interest for a year?

3. How much interest will you earn on $10,000 at 3.5% interest for a year?

4. How much interest will you earn on $750 at 6.9% interest for a year?

5. How much interest will you earn on $5,000 at 7% interest for a year?

36 Compound Interest

I think we're finally ready to learn about compound interest!

If you open a savings account, in the first year you earn interest on the amount you deposited. The next year you earn interest on the full amount in your account—the amount you deposited, plus the interest you earned last year.

So you earn interest on your interest?! Woohoo!

Wow! Your money will grow much more quickly with compound interest!

1. You go into a bank, open a savings account, and deposit $1,000. The account has a 4% interest rate that compounds annually. Use the chart below to calculate how much will be in your account in ten years, assuming that you don't deposit or withdraw money and that you are not charged any fees. Round your answers to one decimal place.

Year	Starting balance	Interest earned	Total
1	$1,000	$1,000 x 0.04 = $40	$1,000 + $40 = $1,040
2	$1,040	$1,040 x 0.04 = $41.60	$1,040 + $41.60 = $1,081.60
3	$1,081.60	$1,081.60 x 0.04 = $43.30	$1,081.60 + $43.30 = $1,124.90
4	$1,124.90	$1,124.90 x 0.04 = $45	$1,124.90 + $45 = $1,169.90
5	$1,169.90	$1,169.90 x 0.04 = $_____	$1,169.90 + $_____ = $_____

What is your total after five years?

How much money will you earn in interest altogether over five years?

2. Now imagine you do the exact same thing at another bank. The only difference is that this bank offers a 6% interest rate. Use the table to calculate the interest you will earn.

Year	Starting balance	Interest earned	Total
1	$1,000	$1,000 x 0.06 = $60	$1,000 + $60 = $1,060
2	$1,060	$1,060 x 0.06 = $63.60	$1,060 + $63.60 = $1,123.60
3	$1,123.60	$1,123.60 x 0.06 = $67.40	$1,123.60 + $67.40 = $1,191
4	$1,191	$1,191 x 0.06 = $71.50	$1,191 + $71.50 = $1,262.50
5	$1,262.50	$1,262.50 x 0.06 = $_____	$1,262.50 + $_____ = $_____

What is your total after five years?

How much money will you earn in interest altogether over five years?

How much more will you earn from the savings account with the higher interest rate?

37 Calculate Compound Interest

+ ◆ ✳ + ◆ ✳ + + ◆ + + + ✳ + + ◆ + ✳ + + ◆ + ✳ + + ◆ + + + ✳ + + ◆ + ✳

Use this formula to calculate compound interest for accounts that compound annually:

Final amount= Principal x (1 + annual interest rate)^{TIME ELAPSED}

1. Calculate the final amount for a savings account that had $200 deposited in it 8 years ago, and earns 7% compound interest annually.

> Use this value: $(1 + 0.07)^8 = (1.07)^8 = 1.72$

$200 \times (1 + 0.07)^8 = \$200 \times (1.07)^8 = \$200 \times 1.72 = \$_____$

2. Calculate the final amount for a savings account that had $600 deposited in it 10 years ago, and earns 6% compound interest annually.

> Use this value: $(1 + 0.06)^{10} = (1.06)^{10} = 1.79$

$600 \times (1 + 0.06)^{10} =$

3. Calculate the final amount for a savings account that had $2,000 deposited in it 15 years ago, and earns 3% compound interest annually.

> Use this value: $(1 + 0.03)^{15} = (1.03)^{15} = 1.56$

$2,000 \times (1 + 0.03)^{15} =$

You can also use the Rule of 72 to estimate how many years it will take to double your money. Let's take a look:

THE RULE OF 72

The Rule of 72 is an easy way to estimate how long it will take to double your money.

72 ÷ interest rate = years to double money

Here's how long it would take to double your money with an interest rate of:

12% ⟶ 6 years
8% ⟶ 9 years
6% ⟶ 12 years
3% ⟶ 24 years
2% ⟶ 36 years

Basically, the rate of increase and the amount of time should multiply to 72 to double your money. If you earn 1% interest, it will take 72 years. For 2% interest, it will take 36 years. For 6% interest, it would take 12 years, because 6 times 12 is 72. This is just an estimation, but it's usually right on the money!

1. Using the rule of 72, how long would it take to double your money given:

   a. 4% interest

   b. 9% interest

   c. 24% interest

38 Inflation

Do you two know what the term "inflation" means?

I'm assuming you don't mean blowing up balloons?

I've heard of it, but I don't know exactly what it means. My parents complain about it a lot though!

Inflation refers to the way that prices go up over time. For example, in 2023 a gallon of milk cost $4.33. But in 1980 it cost $1.12!

Woah! I wish we still had 1980 prices!

Me too! But it's important to remember that salaries were also lower, so it didn't seem so cheap to people back then.

That's good to know. But what exactly does it have to do with saving money?

Well, you can assume that inflation will increase over your lifetime, and everything will cost more when you're older. So, it's another reason why it's important to start saving early, and to make sure you're earning interest on your money.

How much will prices go up?

We don't know the future. There are a lot of complicated factors that determine how prices rise. But we can study the past.

Fill in the chart below. Use the internet to find the prices of these household items and how they have changed over the years.

Item	1980 price	1990 price	2000 price	2010 price	2020 price
A gallon of milk					
A loaf of bread					
A gallon of gas					

I know a website that can help! The Federal Reserve Bank of St Louis Economic Research site has lots of data about how prices have changed over the years. Go to fred.stlouisfed.org or use a search engine to find their website. Then use the search bar on their website to search for the product, like milk.

39 Tracking Inflation

1. Use this chart to record the price of some items at your local grocery store. Hold onto this chart and continue to check the prices over the next few weeks and months. See if any of these prices rise. Make sure that you compare the same brands and the same sizes. Add a few items of your choice to monitor.

Item	Price as of _____ (today's date)	Change noticed
Loaf of bread		
Pound of spaghetti		
Dozen eggs		
Bag of baby carrots		
Pint of chocolate ice cream		
Gallon of milk		
Jar of peanut butter		
Pound of butter		
Laundry detergent		
Dish soap		

2. If all of these items increase in price, how would this affect your budget? Which items would you prioritize buying? Which would you consider buying less frequently?

3. Based on what you know about how prices have increased since 1980, how much do you think these items will cost in 2040?

40 Reflection

What are your current financial needs (things you are responsible for paying for)? What do you anticipate being responsible for in the next few years?

What is most important to you when you think about saving money for the future?

What type of savings account will best help you to save money?

What is a financial goal that you would like to achieve by the time you graduate high school?

How will you go about achieving it?

41 Saving Review

We learned a lot in this chapter! Let's review:

★ **Why it's important to save**

★ **Types of savings accounts**

★ **Simple interest**

★ **Compound interest**

★ **Inflation**

★ **Setting goals**

You've persuaded me! I'm onboard the savings train now.

Advanced Money Managing

I had a lot of expenses at the beginning. I had to pay rent and make the store look nice, with new paint, signs, and decorations.

Plus I had to buy all my inventory!

And you still have a lot of expenses, right?

Sure. I have rent every month. I pay my employees and myself. I have to buy more products, and I have insurance payments too.

Insurance?

Absolutely. Imagine if there was a disaster and something happened to the store. I need to know that I'll be able to afford to fix it.

That's a lot to keep track of. Being a business owner seems a little scary!

It's a lot of work, and it requires some serious skills as far as managing your money goes.

But I'm proud of my store!

43 Credit

First up—let's talk about credit cards. Do either of you have one?

Not yet. I don't know if it's the best idea for me right now. I tend to spend a little too much as it is, although I'm getting better.

I don't. But I think I would use it responsibly if I did.

Credit cards can be a great tool, but you can get into a lot of debt if you're not careful. When you use a credit card, you should keep track of every dollar you spend and make sure you don't spend more than you have. Then pay off your bill in full every month.

What happens if you can't pay it off at the end of the month? Do you get in trouble?

Nope, you're not in trouble. You do have to pay a minimum amount, but you don't have to pay the whole thing. You'll be charged interest on the remaining balance, though. That means you wind up spending way more than you might expect!

But if you pay it off every month, then that's not so bad. But why is it better than a debit card?

Well, having credit and paying it off allows you to build your credit score.

I've heard of that. It's like a report card, but for your money, right?

Sort of. You can have a higher credit score by borrowing money and paying it back. Borrowing money and not paying on time can lower your credit score.

Like if you only pay the minimum amount due?

As long as you pay the minimum amount, it won't generally won't lower your credit score. But if you don't pay anything at all, then your score will go down.

What's so great about these scores anyway?

A better credit score will make it easier to get a credit card. It also makes it easier to get a mortgage or other type of loan in the future. Building your credit score now can be helpful for when you're older and are ready to buy a home or start a business.

But if you're not sure you're responsible enough to pay it off?

In that case, don't do it! Credit cards are helpful when used responsibly, but harmful when they're abused. You can rack up a lot of debt in a short amount of time if you're not careful. And the interest can make it very hard to pay off. It can take a long time to get out of debt.

Well, I'm still interested. I'll keep track of everything I put on my credit card and make sure it's less than I have in my bank account at all times.

44 Calculating Interest on a Loan

There are all sorts of reasons people take out loans—to pay for school, to start a business, to renovate a home, and more—but keep in mind that you aren't just repaying the principal. You must also repay interest. In this activity, we'll use simple interest to estimate how much you would need to pay back on a loan. But keep in mind that in the real world, there are a lot of factors that can complicate these calculations. If you'd like to learn more, there are online calculators that you can use to create different scenarios. For instance, if the interest compounds, you'll need to pay a lot more! This is why you may have heard adults complaining about student loans.

1. a. How much interest will you have to pay on a loan of $2,000 at 4% interest for three years?

$2,000 x 4% x 3 = $_____

b. What is the total amount you will have to pay back on this loan?

$2,000 + $_____ = $_____

2. a. How much interest will you pay on a loan of $300 at 12.3% interest for two years?

b. What is the total amount you will have to pay back on this loan?

$300 + $_____ = $_____

3. a. How much interest will you pay on a loan of $700 at 6.3% interest for five years?

b. What is the total amount you will have to pay back on this loan?

$700 + $_____ = $_____

4. **a.** How much interest will you pay on a loan of $2,000 at 5.5% interest for seven years?

    b. What is the total amount you will have to pay back on this loan?

5. **a.** How much interest will you pay on a loan of $1,500 at 5% interest for three years?

    b. What is the total amount you will have to pay back on this loan?

6. **a.** How much interest will you pay on a loan of $24,000 at 7% interest for five years?

    b. What is the total amount you will have to pay back on this loan?

7. **a.** How much interest will you pay on a loan of $25,500 at 2.75% interest for sixteen years?

    b. What is the total amount you will have to pay back on this loan?

✦✦✦✶✦✦✦✦✦✶✦✦✦✦✶✦✦✦✶✦✦✦✦✶✦✦✦✶✦✦✦✶✦✦✦✶✦✦✦✶✦✦✦✶✦✦✦✶

Credit cards have an APR, or annual percentage rate, that is applied to any outstanding money you owe after each billing period. If you want to calculate how much interest your balance accrues in a month, you divide the APR by 12 and multiply it against your balance. Let's practice calculating interest.

1. Izzie uses her credit card to buy airplane tickets in May. Her credit card payment is due at the end of June. She does not pay her full balance and carries over $500. If her APR is 12%, then how much interest will she accrue for the month of July?

    $500 x (12% ÷ 12) = $500 x 1% = $500 x 0.01 = $5

2. Mima moves into a new apartment and spends $2,000 on things for her new home in October. Her payment is due at the end of November, but she pays only $1,000. If her APR is 12%, how much interest will she accrue by the end of December?

    ($2,000 – $1,000) x (_____% ÷ 12) = $1,000 x 1% =

3. Gordon buys a new bicycle for $210. He makes the minimum monthly payment of $20. How much interest will he accrue in the first month, if his APR is 12%?

($210 – $20) x (_____% ÷ _____) =

4. Xavier spends $1,335 and pays the minimum payment of $35. How much interest will he accrue in the first month, if his APR is 6%?

($1,335 – $35) x (_____% ÷ _____) =

Credit Card Research

1. Use the internet to research credit cards. You can ask an adult to recommend a specific bank or company to focus on. Record their APRs below. Some credit cards may offer a promotion when you sign up that gives you an APR of 0% for a limited amount of time. Record the APR that it will go up to after the introductory period ends.

	Name	APR
Card 1	Sample: Bank of Hannah card	11%
Card 2		
Card 3		

2. Calculate the amount you would pay in interest if you carry a balance of $500 for an entire year. To keep it simple, let's imagine that you are paying your monthly minimums each month, but you also have new charges. So each month you carry over exactly $500.

Card	APR	Interest accrued
Sample: Bank of Hannah card	11%	$55

3. Which of these cards would be the best choice for someone who needs to leave a balance on their credit card? Which would be the worst choice?

4. Are there any other benefits that these credit cards offer? Record them here:

5. Why do you think credit card companies offer promotions to new customers?

I want to learn more about investing.
What are my options? I want to make money!!

Great question! First of all, remember that you will earn interest from money in a savings account. And that's one of the safer ways to earn money from your money. But here are a few more ways. One is to invest in stocks.

Stocks are . . . a share of ownership in a company?

That's right, it means you own a small part of the company! It's called a share, and you can buy shares. Stock prices go up and down depending on how well the company is doing. You want the price of stock to go up after you buy it—that way you make money when you sell it. But of course, you never know for sure what will happen.

Sounds a little risky.

Definitely. I don't think it's bad to try investing a small amount, but don't put too much of your money in stocks. Keep in mind that you could lose money, and don't invest more than you are willing to lose.

What are my other options?

 Mutual funds are a little less risky. They're made up of a collection of assets including stocks, bonds and securities. Having your money invested in different things is called diversification. The more you diversify your investments, the less likely it is that you will lose a lot of money. Even if one of your stocks doesn't perform well, there will probably be others that do well and balance it out.

Is there any disadvantage?

 It's less likely that you'll make a lot of money. You'll probably see more modest returns.

I don't mind a little risk. I'd like to try for a bigger return! I would never invest more than I can afford to lose anyway.

Eh, I'd like to play it a little safer. I work hard for my money!

 Everyone has different preferences and that's fine. Just make sure you don't do anything too risky!

Researching Stocks

1. Pick five companies that you are interested in and look up the price of their stock per share. Keep in mind that not all companies are publicly traded. Private companies don't sell shares. Continue to check their price over the next week and keep track of any changes you see.

 There are many websites you can use to look up prices. You can look at Yahoo Finance, or the websites for the NASDAQ or New York Stock Exchange.

Day	Company 1 AAPL (Apple)	Company 2	Company 3	Company 4	Company 5
1					
2					
3					
4					
5					
6					
7					

2. Which stock performed the best? Which stock performed the worst?

3. If you had purchased ten shares of each stock at the beginning of the week and sold them at the end of the week, how much would you have gained or lost? Use a plus or minus to show whether it is a gain or a loss.

Company	Value on Day 1	Value on Day 7	Gain or Loss?	Amount gained or lost

4. What did you learn from your research? If you were buying stocks, what would your strategy be?

Well friends, we've covered a lot. But there is still one more thing on our syllabus.

Insurance!

By now, I think you two can probably name a few different types of insurance.

Health insurance!

Pet insurance!

Car insurance?

Home insurance!

Spot on! All of these types of insurance basically work in the same way. You know that there is always a risk that something bad could happen. You could get sick, your car could break down, or you could get a leak in your home. Fixing the problem would be very expensive. So to minimize your risk, you pay a small amount each month to an insurance company. Then when you need help, they pay for your doctor's visit, your car repair, or a new roof.

Woohoo! I love insurance!

 Just keep in mind that some plans are better than others. Sometimes your insurance may not cover everything. For example, your health insurance may not cover a trip to the ophthalmologist. Or you might be covered, but you need to pay a deductible first.

A deductible?

 Yup. That's the amount your insurance says you're responsible for paying first, before they will cover the rest. And sometimes it's a lot!

Ok, this is more confusing than I thought.

 It can be confusing. Your plans will come with a lot of details and you need to read the fine print. But it's still good to be insured. You never know what you might need help paying for in the future!

Insurance

+ ◆ + ✦ + ◆ + ✦ + ◆ + ✦ + ◆ + ✦ + ◆ + ✦ + ◆ + ✦ + ◆ + ✦ + ◆ + ✦ + ◆ + ✦

Read the list of scenarios below and write the type of insurance that would cover it.
You can use the internet to research.

1. Getting a cavity filled

2. Getting an injury at a job

3. Repairing the house you own after a storm

4. Bringing your cat to the vet

5. Getting a repair for your car

6. Going to the doctor for a check-up

7. Your belongings being damaged in your rented home

8. Getting a new pair of glasses

Ask your family what types of insurance you have. List them below and record what each type of insurance covers.

51 Advanced Money Managing Review

We learned a lot in this chapter! Let's review:

★ How loans accrue interest

★ How to use credit cards

★ What a credit score is

★ All about investing

★ Types of insurance plans

I'm proud of how much we've learned together! I know there is plenty more that I'll learn as I get older, but I feel much more confident than I did when we started.

Review
and Reflect

52 Review

Try to answer the following questions without referring to previous sections. If you get stuck, reread the section that contains the answer, and then answer in your own words.

1. What are some common things that are deducted from a paycheck? List at least three things and explain what they are. (Earning)

2. What is the difference between gross income and net income? (Earning)

3. What is a retirement account? (Saving)

There are many possible correct answers to these questions. When you are done, review your answers with an adult!

4. What is the difference between a credit card and a debit card? (Spending)

5. How do customers use digital payments? What types of digital payments can you name?

    (Spending)

6. What do you need to write on a personal check? (Spending)

Review

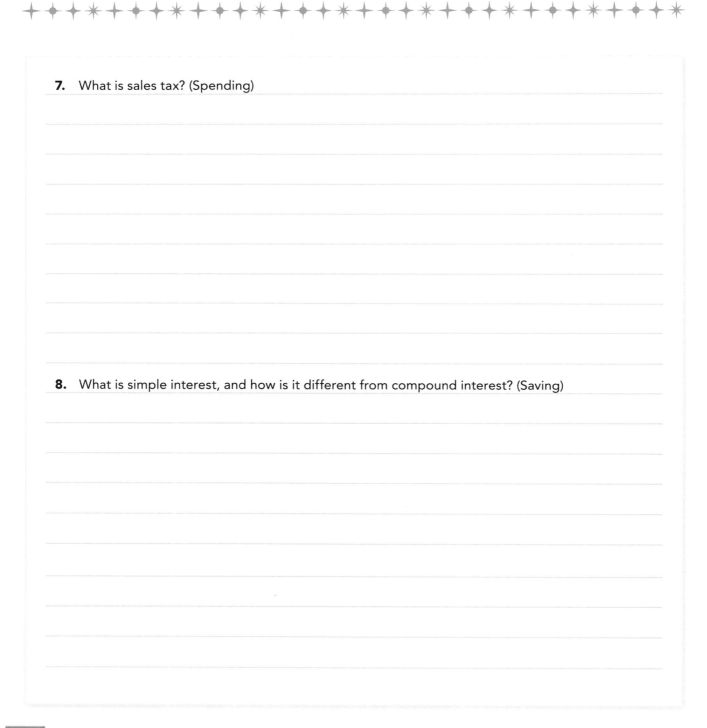

7. What is sales tax? (Spending)

8. What is simple interest, and how is it different from compound interest? (Saving)

9. What is inflation? (Saving)

10. Name two reasons people buy insurance. (Advanced Money Managing)

53 Reflect

+✦+✶+✦+✦+✶+✦+✦+✶+✦+✦+✶+✦+✦+✶+✦+✦+✶+✦+✦+✶+✦+✦+✶+✦+✦+✶

Use the next few pages to reflect on what you learned in this book and how you will apply this knowledge to your own life.

1. What did you learn in this book that most surprised you?

2. How do you use money in your life right now? Do you earn money from a job, or receive an allowance? Do you spend money? Do you save money?

3. What is your biggest priority now when it comes to managing money?

4. What financial needs do you expect to have in the future? How do you plan to pay for these needs?

Reflect

5. It's good to set goals when it comes to money. For instance, you might set a goal of sticking to a budget so that you don't overspend, or you might set a goal to save a certain amount of money by a certain time. Use this space to set a goal for yourself. What will you need to do to achieve this goal?

6. Personal finance is a complicated topic, and you will continue to learn about it as you get older. What are you still curious about? List some questions you have below.

7. Make a plan with an adult to find the answers to these questions. Where will you go to find

    the answers? Who do you know that can help answer your questions? Record your plan here.

Reflect

8. Do you have any regrets about how you have spent money in the past? Write a letter to your past self and share what lessons you have learned.

Glossary

Glossary

401k	(noun)	a retirement account provided by a job to its employees as a benefit
Accrue	(verb)	earn or grow
APR (annual percentage rate)	(noun)	the amount a credit card charges you when you carry over an outstanding balance
Benefit	(noun)	something provided to an employee by their employer in addition to their salary or wage, such as health insurance
Budget	(noun)	a tool that is used to plan expenses
CDs (Certificates of Deposit)	(noun)	a type of account that you leave money in for a set amount of time. The money earns interest, but cannot be withdrawn early.
Check	(noun)	a slip of paper that allows you to send money from one bank account to another
Commission	(noun)	money paid to someone for performing a service
Credit card	(noun)	a card that allows a person to make purchases and pay for them later
Credit score	(noun)	a number assigned to lenders that reflects how much banks trust them to pay back money that is borrowed

Debit card	(noun)	a card that allows a person to make purchases using funds in their checking account
Deductible	(noun)	the amount that an insurance company requires an individual to pay before covering the remaining balance
Deposit	(verb)	to put something away
Digital payments	(noun)	ways of paying for things using a phone, smart watch, or similar device
Direct deposit	(noun)	a method businesses use to pay employees that involves placing money directly into their bank account
Discount	(noun)	a reduced price
Diversification	(noun)	the practice of investing money in different things to minimize risk
Dividend	(noun)	a profit that is shared with a stockholder
Fee	(noun)	an amount that is charged
Fixed expenses	(noun)	expenses of the same amount and frequency each month, which can be easily predicted

Glossary

Gross income	(noun)	the amount of money you earn before taxes or anything else is deducted
Hourly wage	(noun)	an amount of money paid to a worker based on the amount of time worked
Income tax	(noun)	a tax paid on one's gross income
Inflation	(noun)	a term that describes the way that prices increase over time
Insurance	(noun)	a business which collects money from customers and promises to cover their expenses in the event of a specified event
Invest	(verb)	to commit money to something in order to earn more money
Loan	(noun)	money that is borrowed and accrues interest
Minimum wage	(noun)	the lowest amount a business can legally pay their employees
Money Market account	(noun)	a type of savings account that earns interest, but allows you to access funds with a debit card or check
Mutual funds	(noun)	a collection of assets including stocks, bonds, and securities

Net income	(noun)	the amount you actually earn after taxes and other deductions are subtracted from your gross pay
Paid time off	(noun)	a benefit that employees receive where they can take a certain amount of time off from their job without losing pay
Pay period	(noun)	the amount of time a paycheck compensates an employee for
Principal	(noun)	the amount of money an account or a loan starts with, which can earn interest
Retail	(noun)	goods that are sold
Retirement account	(noun)	a bank account that offers customers interest and some tax advantages if they leave their money in the account until retirement
Roth IRA	(noun)	an individual savings account for retirement
Salary	(noun)	an amount of money an employee is paid in a year
Sales tax	(noun)	a tax that customers pay when spending money
Saving account	(noun)	a bank account that offers interest

Glossary

Share	(noun)	a portion of a company's stock which can be purchased
Shift	(noun)	scheduled work hours
Social Security	(noun)	a government program designed to help retirees and people who are disabled
Stock	(noun)	a share of a public company that can be purchased by investors
Tax	(noun)	money collected by the government
Tip	(noun)	money that a customer leaves a service worker in appreciation

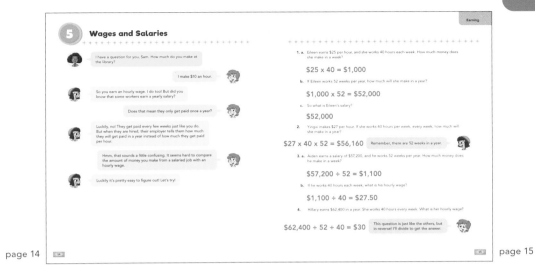

5 Wages and Salaries

Earning

I have a question for you, Sam. How much do you make at the library?

I make $10 an hour.

So you earn an hourly wage. I do too! But did you know that some workers earn a yearly salary?

Does that mean they only get paid once a year?

Luckily, no! They get paid every few weeks just like you do. But when they are hired, their employer tells them how much they will get paid in a year instead of how much they get paid per hour.

Hmm, that sounds a little confusing. It seems hard to compare the amount of money you make from a salaried job with an hourly wage.

Luckily it's pretty easy to figure out! Let's try!

1. a. Eileen earns $25 per hour, and she works 40 hours each week. How much money does she make in a week?

$25 x 40 = $1,000

b. If Eileen works 52 weeks per year, how much will she make in a year?

$1,000 x 52 = $52,000

c. So what is Eileen's salary?

$52,000

2. Yinga makes $27 per hour. If she works 40 hours per week, every week, how much will she make in a year?

$27 x 40 x 52 = $56,160   Remember, there are 52 weeks in a year.

3. a. Aiden earns a salary of $57,200, and he works 52 weeks per year. How much money does he make in a week?

$57,200 ÷ 52 = $1,100

b. If he works 40 hours each week, what is his hourly wage?

$1,100 ÷ 40 = $27.50

4. Hillary earns $62,400 in a year. She works 40 hours every week. What is her hourly wage?

$62,400 ÷ 52 ÷ 40 = $30   This question is just like the others, but in reverse! I'll divide to get the answer.

6 Calculating with Pay Periods

Earning

1. Eliza makes $93,600 per year. If her job pays her every two weeks, how much does she make each time she gets paid?

52 weeks in a year divided by two weeks= **26** weeks
(This is the number of pay periods per year.)

$93,600 ÷ **26** = $**3,600** every two weeks

2. Sera earns $39,000 each year. If she is paid every two weeks, how much does she make each pay period?

52 ÷ 2 = 26
39,000 ÷ 26 = $1,500

3. Richard earns $54,000 each year. If he is paid twice per month, how much does he make each pay period?

12 months x 2 = **24** pay periods per year

$54,000 ÷ **24** = $**2,250** each pay period

Each job can set their own pay periods. Most jobs pay their employees every two weeks (26 paychecks in a year) or twice per month (24 paychecks in a year). But some may pay every week or once a month. You have to ask when you start a new job.

4. Sinclair earns $113,000 per year. If he is paid twice per year, how much does he make each pay period?

113,000 ÷ 2 = $56,500

5. Maureen gets paid $3,230 twice per month. What is her annual salary?

$3,230 x (12 x 2) = $3,230 x 24 = $77,520

6. Lin gets paid $500 every other week. What is her annual salary?

$500 x (52 ÷ 2) = $500 x 26 = $13,000

7. Thom gets paid $2,700 twice per month. What is his annual salary?

$2,700 x (12 x 2) = $2,700 x 24 = $64,800

8. Frank gets paid $2,160 every other week. What is his annual salary?

$2,160 x (52 ÷ 2) = $2,160 x 26 = $56,160

7 Wages with Tip and Commission

Earning

Ok, now I have a question. You earn tips at work, right?

That's correct!

So how do you calculate how much you earn each week?

Great question! I never know exactly how much I'll earn, but I have a pretty good estimate. I know how much I make, so that part is easy. I don't know what my tips will be—that can vary a lot depending on how busy we are and how generous the customers are that day! But I keep track of how much I earn, so I can calculate the average amount. Although the amount I receive varies day to day, knowing the average helps me to have an idea of what to expect.

Oh man, I think I need to see an example.

I earn $15 an hour. That's the minimum wage for all employees in this state, which means that everyone here must earn at least $15 per hour. Last week I made $30 in tips on Monday, $20 on Wednesday, and $40 on Saturday. That adds up to a total of $90 for three shifts. And if I divide $90 by three, then I know that I make an average of $30 in tips each shift.

Ok, that makes sense.

And here's one more thing that can affect your pay check: commissions. When my employees make a sale, I pay them 5% of the sale as a commission. Let's try calculating some examples together.

1. Tory makes $15/hour in a bagel shop and earns an average of $45 in tips each shift. How much will she earn in a week where she works two shifts, and each shift is eight hours?
Wage: 8 hours x 2 = **16** hours. $15 x **16** hours = $**240**
Tips: $45 x 2 = $**90**
Total: $**240** + $**90** = $**330**

2. Sunita makes $10/hour in a restaurant and earns an average of $130 in tips each shift. How much will she earn in a week where she works four shifts, and each shift is seven hours?
Wage: 7 hours x 4 = 28 hours. $10 x 28 hours = $280
Tips: $130 x 4 = $520
Total: $280 + $520 = $800

3. Taylor works in a clothing store. He earns $17 an hour and works 40 hours a week. He earns 5% commission on his sales. How much will he make in a week where he sells $1,200 worth of clothing?
Wage: $17 x 40 = $**680**
Commission: $1,200 x 5% = $1,200 x 0.05 = $**60**
Total: $**680** + $**60** = $**740**

4. Stephanie earns $13 an hour at a shoe store and works 35 hours a week. She makes 7% commission on each pair of shoes she sells. How much does she make in a week where she sells $2,000 worth of shoes?
Wage: $13 x 35 = $455
Commission: $2,000 x 7% = $2,000 x 0.07 = $140
Total: $455 + $140 = $595

Each state sets their own minimum wage, so the minimum wage varies depending on where you live. And keep in mind: some employees can be paid less than minimum wage—as long as they are receiving tips! For example, if the minimum wage is $15 per hour in your state, you could be paid $10 an hour from your employer. As long as you receive at least $5 in tips each hour, you will still get $15 an hour, which is why this is allowed. This is very common in restaurants.

8 Calculating Wages

1. Earnest is paid $9.50 an hour at a restaurant. This week, he works an 8-hour shift, a 7-hour shift, and two 7.5-hour shifts. He earns the following in tips: $65, $54, $85, and $87.

   a. How much does he earn this week?

   Wage: $9.50 × 8 + $9.50 × 7 + $9.50 × 7.5 + $9.50 × 7.5 = $285

   Tips: $65 + $54 + $85 + $87 = $291

   Total: $285 + $291 = $576

   b. What does he average in tips per shift?

   $291 ÷ 4 shifts = $72.75

2. Samantha is paid $8.75 an hour at a restaurant. In one week, she works two 9-hour shifts, a 7-hour shift, and two 8.5-hour shifts. She earns the following in tips: $94, $110, $63, $44, and $77.

   a. How much does she earn this week?

   Wage: $8.75 × 9 + $8.75 × 9 + $8.75 × 7 + $8.75 × 8.5 + $8.75 × 8.5
   = $8.75 × (9 + 9 + 7 + 8.5 + 8.5) = $8.75 × 42 = $367.50

   Tips: $94 + $110 + $63 + $44 + $77 = $388

   Total: $367.50 + $388 = $755.50

   b. What does she average in tips per shift?

   $388 ÷ 5 = $77.60

3. Ellie is paid $9.85 an hour at a café. In one week, she works two 8-hour shifts and two 8.5-hour shifts. She earns the following in tips: $64, $70, $83, and $71.

   a. How much does she earn this week?

   Wage: $9.85 × 8 + $9.85 × 8 + $9.85 × 8.5 + $9.85 × 8.5
   = $9.85 × (8 + 8 + 8.5 + 8.5) = $9.85 × 33 = $325.05

   Tips: $64 + $70 + $83 + $71 = $288

   Total: $325.05 + $288 = $613.05

   b. What does she average in tips per shift?

   $288 ÷ 4 = $72

4. Tim is paid $10.50 an hour at a coffee shop. In one week, he works two 8-hour shifts, a 7.5-hour shift, and two 6.5-hour shifts. He earns the following in tips: $67, $84, $89, $71, and $82.

   a. How much does he earn this week?

   Wage: $10.50 × 8 + $10.50 × 8 + $10.50 × 7.5 + $10.50 × 6.5 + $10.50 × 6.5 = $10.50 × (8 + 8 + 7.5 + 6.5 + 6.5) = $10.50 × 36.5 = $383.25

   Tips: $67 + $84 + $89 + $71 + $82 = $393

   Total: $383.25 + $393 = $776.25

   b. What does he average in tips per shift?

   $393 ÷ 5 = $78.60

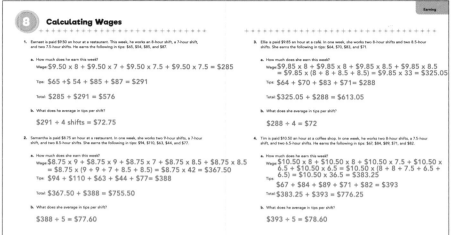

9 Income Tax

Ok, here's a question—why do I always get less money than I think I will? When I calculate how much I make, I get one number. But when the paycheck comes, it's a completely different number. And it's way lower!

Yes! That's because of taxes. And other stuff . . . Honestly, this gets pretty complicated, so I'm going to need Hannah to explain.

Let's talk about taxes first. Everyone pays income taxes to the federal government, and in most states, you are also taxed on your income. Some places even have a local tax. Your taxes are a percentage of your income, and they are based on the amount you earn in a year. It's a little complicated to calculate. We'll look at some examples together so that you can get a sense of how it works.

Ugh, why do I even have to pay taxes? It's so unfair.

Well, our government needs the money to pay its employees and to build things for the public like schools and roads. But no one enjoys seeing that money come out of their paycheck! The important thing is to remember that these taxes exist, and to keep them in mind when you're planning.

So how do you know how much to pay?

Luckily your employer will do the math for you! And it's tricky. You pay a percentage that increases as you make more money.

I have a question. I hear everyone complain about paying taxes in April. But it seems like we pay taxes all year round!

Great point. If you are earning money, you have to file taxes every year in April. That means filling out paperwork, and it's not fun! But if your job has been deducting taxes from your paycheck all year, then you'll probably find that you don't owe any money—or at least not much. It's even possible that you may have overpaid, and you might get a refund check!

Yes please!

1. Imagine you live in Seattle. You earn $40,000 a year and you pay federal taxes only. Let's see how much you would earn in a two-week period. Round your answer to two decimal places.

   Lucky for us, there is no state tax in Washington! So we only have to worry about federal tax in this problem.

   $40,000 ÷ 26 (since there are 52 weeks in a year, there are 26 two-week periods in a year)
   - $1,538.46 per week.

   Federal tax = You will be taxed on ten percent of the first $11,000 you earn, and twelve percent on the rest of your income. Determine:

   A. 10% of $11,000 ($ 1,100);

   B. 12% of the difference between $40,000 and $11,000.

   $40,000 – $11,000 = $ 29,000 Multiply by 0.12 to get $ 3,480

   Add A + B to get your federal taxes for the year: $ 4,580

   Divide by 26 to get the amount for a two week period: $ 176.15

   Subtract it from the total you earn in a two week period: $ 1362.31

   Phew! I told you it was tricky. Luckily most jobs do this math for you. You only need to figure this out if you are self-employed and don't have a boss!

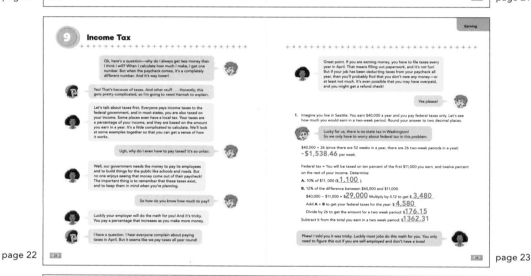

10 Social Security

There's something else you might have noticed on your paycheck. Social Security! It's also referred to as FICA, or Federal Insurance Contributions Act.

Yes, I've seen it before. What is it, exactly? More taxes?

Well, it might feel like a tax in the sense that it comes out of your paycheck and helps contribute to something that benefits everyone. But it's different from income tax.

That's right! Social Security is a program that collects payments from people who are currently working. Then when you are older, you receive payments from Social Security that help you pay for things after you retire.

How old do you have to be to get Social Security payments?

Right now the earliest age is 62. So you have a long ways to go! Although, people with disabilities who are over 18 can receive Social Security benefits if they are not able to work.

Should we look at some examples?

1. Cynthia earns $52,000 per year. Employees pay 6.2% of their income to Social Security. How much does Cynthia pay for Social Security in a two-week period? (Remember that there are 52 weeks in year.)

   $52,000 ÷ (52 ÷ 2) = $52,000 26 = $ 2,000
   $ 2,000 × 6.2% = $ 2,000 × 0.062 = $ 124

Everyone pays 6.2% of their income to Social Security unless they earn more than the limit. In 2023, that amount is $160,200. If you earn more than that, you are still only paying 6.2% of $160,200. So if you earn $200,000, you are only paying 6.2% of $160,200, and not 6.2% of $200,000.

2. Dante earns $135,200 per year. How much does he pay for Social Security in a two-week period?

   $135,200 ÷ (52 ÷ 2) = $135,200 ÷ 26 = $5,200
   $5,200 × 6.2% = $5,200 × 0.062 = $322.40

3. Fatima earns $78,000 per year. How much does she pay for Social Security in a month?

   $78,000 ÷ 12 = $6,500
   $6,500 × 6.2% = $6,500 × 0.062 = $403

4. Alicia earns $35 per hour. If she works 40 hours per week, how much does she pay for Social Security in a week?

   $35 × 40 = $1,400
   $1,400 × 6.2% = $1,400 × 0.062 = $86.80

5. Santos earns $40 per hour and works 35 hours per week. How much does he pay for Social Security in a two-week period?

   $40 × 35 = $1,400
   $1,400 × 6.2% = $1,400 × 0.062 = $86.80
   $86.80 × 2 = $173.60

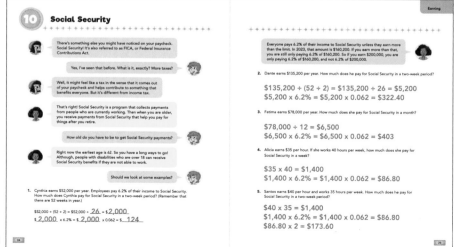

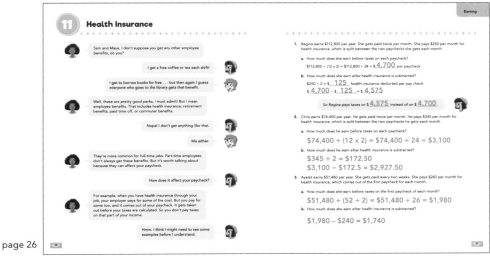

11 Health Insurance

Sam and Maya, I don't suppose you get any other employee benefits, do you?

I get a free coffee or tea each shift!

I get to borrow books for free . . . but then again I guess everyone who goes to the library gets that benefit.

Well, those are pretty good perks, I must admit! But I mean employee benefits. That includes health insurance, retirement benefits, paid time off, or commuter benefits.

Nope! I don't get anything like that.

Me either.

They're more common for full-time jobs. Part-time employees don't always get these benefits. But it's worth talking about because they can affect your paycheck.

How does it affect your paycheck?

For example, when you have health insurance through your job, your employer pays for some of the cost. But you pay for some too, and it comes out of your paycheck. It gets taken out before your taxes are calculated. So you don't pay taxes on that part of your income.

Hmm. I think I might need to see some examples before I understand.

page 26

1. Regina earns $112,800 per year. She gets paid twice per month. She pays $250 per month for health insurance, which is split between the two paychecks she gets each month.
   a. How much does she earn before taxes on each paycheck?
      $112,800 ÷ (12 x 2) = $112,800 ÷ 24 = $ 4,700 per paycheck
   b. How much does she earn after health insurance is subtracted?
      $250 ÷ 2 = $ 125 health insurance deducted per pay check
      $ 4,700 – $ 125 = $ 4,575

So Regina pays taxes on $ 4,575 instead of on $ 4,700.

2. Chris earns $74,400 per year. He gets paid twice per month. He pays $345 per month for health insurance, which is split between the two paychecks he gets each month.
   a. How much does he earn before taxes on each paycheck?
      $74,400 ÷ (12 x 2) = $74,400 ÷ 24 = $3,100
   b. How much does he earn after health insurance is subtracted?
      $345 ÷ 2 = $172.50
      $3,100 – $172.5 = $2,927.50
3. Ayelet earns $51,480 per year. She gets paid every two weeks. She pays $240 per month for health insurance, which comes out of the first paycheck for each month.
   a. How much does she earn before taxes on the first paycheck of each month?
      $51,480 ÷ (52 ÷ 2) = $51,480 ÷ 26 = $1,980
   b. How much does she earn after health insurance is subtracted?
      $1,980 – $240 = $1,740

page 27

12 Retirement Accounts

So, we've already discussed health insurance. Retirement accounts work similarly. Your employer will set up a retirement account for you where you can save money for your retirement. Your employer may contribute some money to this account, but mostly it is a place for you to put your savings. That money comes out of your paycheck, and it also comes out before taxes.

Why is it called a retirement account?

Because the money you put in there should be saved until you retire. If you withdraw your money early, you will have to pay tax plus a penalty. So it's best to leave it there.

What about commuter benefits?

Great question. Some jobs allow you to put aside the money you spend commuting to work into a separate account. Then you can use it to buy bus tickets or whatever else you need. And—you guessed it—that money is taken out before taxes too. So it's another way to reduce the amount of income tax you have to pay.

And what about this "paid time off?"

That means you still get paid when you go on vacation. Most full-time employees get a certain amount of vacation days each year, and sick days too. That way when you need to take time off, your paycheck stays the same. You won't earn less than usual, even though you worked less.

Sign me up for that one!

page 28

1. Francis earns $67,200 per year. She gets paid twice per month. She puts $250 into her retirement account each month, which is split between the two paychecks she gets each month.
   a. How much does she earn before taxes on each paycheck?
      $67,200 ÷ (12 x 2) = $67,200 ÷ 24 = $ 2,800 per paycheck
   b. How much does she earn after her retirement contribution is subtracted?
      $250 ÷ 2 = $ 125 retirement contribution per paycheck
      $ 2,800 – $ 125 = $ 2,675

I've got this one. Francis pays taxes on $ 2,675 instead of on $ 2,800.

2. Mike earns $55,200 per year. He gets paid twice per month. He puts 7% of his income into his retirement account.
   a. How much does he earn before taxes on each paycheck?
      $55,200 ÷ (12 x 2) = $55,200 ÷ 24 = $2,300
   b. How much does he earn after his retirement contribution is subtracted?
      $2,300 x 7% = $2,300 x 0.07 = $161
      $2,300 – $161 = $2,139
      You can also do this: $2,300 x (100% – 7%) = $2,300 x 93% = $2,139
3. Tom earns $75,400 per year. He gets paid every two weeks. He puts $400 each month into his retirement account, which comes out of the first paycheck for each month.
   a. How much does he earn before taxes on the first paycheck of each month?
      $75,400 ÷ (52 ÷ 2) = $75,400 ÷ 26 = $2,900
   b. How much does he earn after subtracting his retirement contribution?
      $2,900 – $400 = $2,500

page 29

13 Gross Income and Net Income

Ok, guys! We've talked about all of the things that get deducted from your paycheck separately. Now I want to put it all together. It's time to talk about gross income and net income.

Excuse you! My income is not gross!

Sam! Gross has more than one meaning!

Your gross income is the amount you make before taxes, Social Security, health insurance, retirement savings . . . all that good stuff. It's the big number you see before all of those things get subtracted.

So net income is the amount you actually get?

Exactly. Your net income is the income you receive once everything has been deducted.

And those numbers can be pretty different. I'm always surprised by how big the difference can be.

Yup! And it's why you should always budget your spending using your net income—we'll discuss that more later.

First we'll look at some examples, right?

You know it!

page 30

1. Myra earns $65,000 per year. She is paid every two weeks, and puts 3% of each paycheck into her retirement account. She lives in Los Angeles and pays state and federal taxes. Search online for a California income tax calculator, and use that to calculate her taxes and what is left over afterwards. Round to the nearest two decimal places.

Go online and search for the keywords "income tax calculator California." That will calculate taxes, including Social Security. Then you can subtract other benefits (like her retirement contribution) yourself.

   $65,000 ÷ (52 ÷ 2) = $65,000 ÷ 26 = $2,500
   ($2,500 x 3%) x 26 = ($2,500 x 0.03) x 26 = $1950
   Federal tax = $6,639
   State tax = $2,265
   FICA tax = $4,973
   Net income = $49,173
2. If Myra made $75,000 per year, with no other change, what would her net income be? How much greater would it be than her income in #1? Round to the nearest two decimal places.
   $75,000 ÷ (52 ÷ 2) = $75,000 ÷ 26 = $2884.61
   ($2884.61 x 3%) x 26 = ($2884.61 x 0.03) x 26 = $2250
   Federal tax = $8773
   State tax = $3,060
   FICA tax = $5,738
   Net income = $55,179

page 31

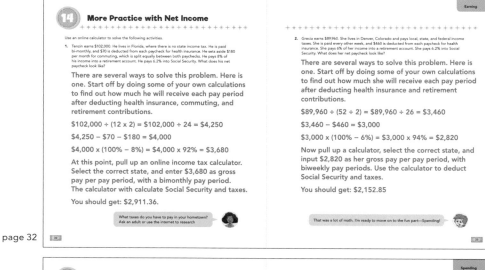

14 · More Practice with Net Income

Use an online calculator to solve the following activities.

1. Tenzin earns $102,000. He lives in Florida, where there is no state income tax. He is paid bi-monthly, and $70 is deducted from each paycheck for health insurance. He sets aside $180 per month for commuting, which is split equally between both paychecks. He pays 8% of his income into a retirement account. He pays 6.2% into Social Security. What does his net paycheck look like?

There are several ways to solve this problem. Here is one. Start off by doing some of your own calculations to find out how much he will receive each pay period after deducting health insurance, commuting, and retirement contributions.

$102,000 ÷ (12 x 2) = $102,000 ÷ 24 = $4,250

$4,250 − $70 − $180 = $4,000

$4,000 x (100% − 8%) = $4,000 x 92% = $3,680

At this point, pull up an online income tax calculator. Select the correct state, and enter $3,680 as gross pay per pay period, with a bimonthly pay period. The calculator with calculate Social Security and taxes.

You should get: $2,911.36.

What taxes do you have to pay in your hometown? Ask an adult or use the internet to research

2. Grecia earns $89,960. She lives in Denver, Colorado and pays local, state, and federal income taxes. She is paid every other week, and $460 is deducted from each paycheck for health insurance. She pays 6% of her income into a retirement account. She pays 6.2% into Social Security. What does her net paycheck look like?

There are several ways to solve this problem. Here is one. Start off by doing some of your own calculations to find out how much she will receive each pay period after deducting health insurance and retirement contributions.

$89,960 ÷ (52 ÷ 2) = $89,960 ÷ 26 = $3,460

$3,460 − $460 = $3,000

$3,000 x (100% − 6%) = $3,000 x 94% = $2,820

Now pull up a calculator, select the correct state, and input $2,820 as her gross pay per pay period, with biweekly pay periods. Use the calculator to deduct Social Security and taxes.

You should get: $2,152.85

That was a lot of math. I'm ready to move on to the fun part—Spending!

page 32 · page 33

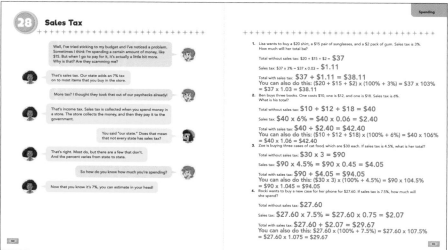

28 · Sales Tax

Well, I've tried sticking to my budget and I've noticed a problem. Sometimes I think I'm spending a certain amount of money, like $15. But when I go to pay for it, it's actually a little bit more. Why is that? Are they scamming me?

That's sales tax. Our state adds an 7% tax on to most items that you buy in the store.

More tax? I thought they took that out of our paychecks already!

That's income tax. Sales tax is collected when you spend money in a store. The store collects the money, and then they pay it to the government.

You said "our state." Does that mean that not every state has sales tax?

That's right. Most do, but there are a few that don't. And the percent varies from state to state.

So how do you know how much you're spending?

Now that you know it's 7%, you can estimate in your head!

1. Lisa wants to buy a $20 shirt, a $15 pair of sunglasses, and a $2 pack of gum. Sales tax is 3%. How much will her total be?

Total without sales tax: $20 + $15 + $2 = **$37**

Sales tax: $37 x 3% = $37 x 0.03 = **$1.11**

Total with sales tax: **$37 + $1.11 = $38.11**
You can also do this: ($20 + $15 + $2) x (100% + 3%) = $37 x 103% = $37 x 1.03 = $38.11

2. Ben buys three books. One costs $10, one is $12, and one is $18. Sales tax is 6%. What is his total?

Total without sales tax: **$10 + $12 + $18 = $40**

Sales tax: $40 x 6% = $40 x 0.06 = **$2.40**

Total with sales tax: **$40 + $2.40 = $42.40**
You can also do this: ($10 + $12 + $18) x (100% + 6%) = $40 x 106% = $40 x 1.06 = $42.40

3. Zoe is buying three cases of cat food, which are $30 each. If sales tax is 4.5%, what is her total?

Total without sales tax: **$30 x 3 = $90**

Sales tax: $90 x 4.5% = $90 x 0.45 = **$4.05**

Total with sales tax: **$90 + $4.05 = $94.05**
You can also do this: ($30 x 3) x (100% + 4.5%) = $90 x 104.5% = $90 x 1.045 = $94.05

4. Rocki wants to buy a new case for her phone for $27.60. If sales tax is 7.5%, how much will she spend?

Total without sales tax: **$27.60**

Sales tax: $27.60 x 7.5% = $27.60 x 0.75 = **$2.07**

Total with sales tax: **$27.60 + $2.07 = $29.67**
You can also do this: $27.60 x (100% + 7.5%) = $27.60 x 107.5% = $27.60 x 1.075 = $29.67

page 60 · page 61

---

29 · Here's a Tip

I had a difficult day at work today.

I'm sorry to hear that. What went wrong?

There were a lot of demanding customers. So many complaints. And then we barely even got any tips!

Ugh, that is the worst! Sometimes people just don't realize how important tips are to employees.

Can I be honest? Sometimes I'm not sure if I'm tipping well or not. It gets confusing!

It can be a little confusing! Especially because tipping is a custom, and it is different in so many places. In some countries, like Japan, people don't tip at all. In many European countries, people leave small tips. But in the United States, tipping is an important part of an employee's compensation.

Basically, in the United States you should always tip in a restaurant or café. You also tip hairdressers, cab drivers, and delivery people. Oh, and if you get a manicure you have to tip also! You never need to tip in a store, even when an employee helps you find something. But otherwise, you are usually expected to tip anyone whose job involves serving you in some way.

Ok, I think I've got all that. But how much do you tip? Is it 20%?

20% is a standard tip for good service. When in doubt, leave 20%. It's also a nice round number that is pretty easy to calculate in your head.

But here's the thing . . . do I really have to? What happens if I don't?

Then the employees who help you don't make as much money. We count on those tips, Sam! You need to factor them in when you are budgeting how much you will spend at a restaurant. You should leave a 20% tip.

Ok, ok! I get it now.

Calculate the appropriate tip and total for each bill.

1. Restaurant $60
   Tip: $60 x 20% = $60 x 0.2 = $ __12__
   Total: $60 + $ __12__ = $ __72__

2. Hair salon $55
   Tip: $55 x 20% = $55 x 0.2 = $11
   Total: $55 + $11 = $66

3. Taxi $25
   Tip: $25 x 20% = $25 x 0.2 = $5
   Total: $25 + $5 = $30

4. Café $27
   Tip: $27 x 20% = $27 x 0.2 = $5.40
   Total: $27 + $5.40 = $32.40

5. Restaurant $44
   Tip: $44 x 20% = $44 x 0.2 = $8.80
   Total: $44 + $8.80 = $52.80

6. Nail salon $32
   Tip: $32 x 20% = $32 x 0.2 = $6.40
   Total: $32 + $6.40 = $38.40

7. Food delivery $18
   Tip: $18 x 20% = $18 x 0.2 = $3.60
   Total: $18 + $3.60 = $21.60

page 62 · page 63

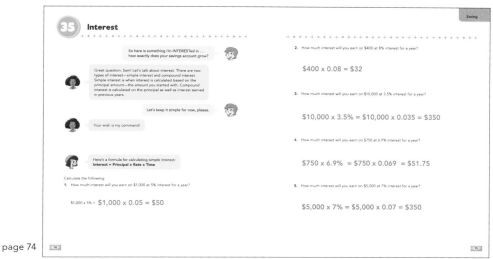

35 Interest

Saving

So here is something I'm INTERESTed in . . . how exactly does your savings account grow?

Great question, Sam! Let's talk about interest. There are two types of interest—simple interest and compound interest. Simple interest is when interest is calculated based on the principal amount—the amount you started with. Compound interest is calculated on the principal as well as interest earned in previous years.

Let's keep it simple for now, please.

Your wish is my command!

Here's a formula for calculating simple interest:
Interest = Principal x Rate x Time

Calculate the following:

1. How much interest will you earn on $1,000 at 5% interest for a year?

$1,000 x 5% = **$1,000 x 0.05 = $50**

2. How much interest will you earn on $400 at 8% interest for a year?

$400 x 0.08 = $32

3. How much interest will you earn on $10,000 at 3.5% interest for a year?

$10,000 x 3.5% = $10,000 x 0.035 = $350

4. How much interest will you earn on $750 at 6.9% interest for a year?

$750 x 6.9% = $750 x 0.069 = $51.75

5. How much interest will you earn on $5,000 at 7% interest for a year?

$5,000 x 7% = $5,000 x 0.07 = $350

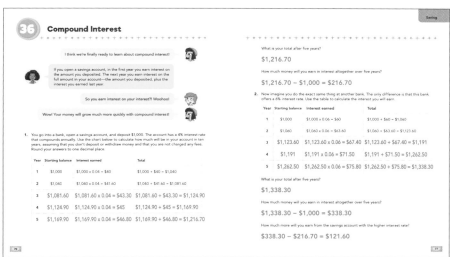

36 Compound Interest

Saving

I think we're finally ready to learn about compound interest!

If you open a savings account, in the first year you earn interest on the amount you deposited. The next year you earn interest on the full amount in your account—the amount you deposited, plus the interest you earned last year.

So you earn interest on your interest?! Woohoo!

Wow! Your money will grow much more quickly with compound interest!

1. You go into a bank, open a savings account, and deposit $1,000. The account has a 4% interest rate that compounds annually. Use the chart below to calculate how much will be in your account in ten years, assuming that you don't deposit or withdraw money and that you are not charged any fees. Round your answers to one decimal place.

Year	Starting balance	Interest earned	Total
1	$1,000	$1,000 x 0.04 = $40	$1,000 + $40 = $1,040
2	$1,040	$1,040 x 0.04 = $41.60	$1,040 + $41.60 = $1,081.60
3	$1,081.60	$1,081.60 x 0.04 = $43.30	$1,081.60 + $43.30 = $1,124.90
4	$1,124.90	$1,124.90 x 0.04 = $45	$1,124.90 + $45 = $1,169.90
5	$1,169.90	$1,169.90 x 0.04 = $46.80	$1,169.90 + $46.80 = $1,216.70

What is your total after five years?

$1,216.70

How much money will you earn in interest altogether over five years?

$1,216.70 − $1,000 = $216.70

2. Now imagine you do the exact same thing at another bank. The only difference is that this bank offers a 6% interest rate. Use the table to calculate the interest you will earn.

Year	Starting balance	Interest earned	Total
1	$1,000	$1,000 x 0.06 = $60	$1,000 + $60 = $1,060
2	$1,060	$1,060 x 0.06 = $63.60	$1,060 + $63.60 = $1,123.60
3	$1,123.60	$1,123.60 x 0.06 = $67.40	$1,123.60 + $67.40 = $1,191
4	$1,191	$1,191 x 0.06 = $71.50	$1,191 + $71.50 = $1,262.50
5	$1,262.50	$1,262.50 x 0.06 = $75.80	$1,262.50 + $75.80 = $1,338.30

What is your total after five years?

$1,338.30

How much money will you earn in interest altogether over five years?

$1,338.30 − $1,000 = $338.30

How much more will you earn from the savings account with the higher interest rate?

$338.30 − $216.70 = $121.60

37 Calculate Compound Interest

Saving

Use this formula to calculate compound interest for accounts that compound annually:
Final amount= Principal x (1 + annual interest rate)$^{\text{TIME ELAPSED}}$

1. Calculate the final amount for a savings account that had $200 deposited in it 8 years ago, and earns 7% compound interest annually.

Use this value: $(1 + 0.07)^8 = (1.07)^8 = 1.72$

$$\$200 \times (1 + 0.07)^8 = \$200 \times (1.07)^8 =$$
$$\$200 \times 1.72 = \$344$$

2. Calculate the final amount for a savings account that had $600 deposited in it 10 years ago, and earns 6% compound interest annually.

Use this value: $(1 + 0.06)^{10} = (1.06)^{10} = 1.79$

$$\$600 \times (1 + 0.06)^{10} = \$600 \times (1.06)^{10} =$$
$$\$600 \times 1.79 = \$1,074$$

3. Calculate the final amount for a savings account that had $2,000 deposited in it 15 years ago, and earns 3% compound interest annually.

Use this value: $(1 + 0.03)^{15} = (1.03)^{15} = 1.56$

$$\$2,000 \times (1 + 0.03)^{15} = \$2,000 \times (1.03)^{15} =$$
$$\$2,000 \times 1.56 = \$3,120$$

You can also use the Rule of 72 to estimate how many years it will take to double your money. Let's take a look:

THE RULE OF 72

The Rule of 72 is an easy way to estimate how long it will take to double your money.
72 ÷ interest rate = years to double money
Here's how long it would take to double your money with an interest rate of:

12%	6 years
8%	9 years
6%	12 years
3%	24 years
2%	36 years

Basically, the rate of increase and the amount of time should multiply to 72 to double your money. If you earn 1% interest, it will take 72 years. For 2% interest, it will take 36 years. For 6% interest, it would take 12 years, because 6 times 12 is 72. This is just an estimation, but it's usually right on the money!

1. Using the rule of 72, how long would it take to double your money given:

a. 4% interest

72 ÷ 4 = 18 years

b. 9% interest

72 ÷ 9 = 8 years

c. 24% interest

72 ÷ 24 = 3 years

44 Calculating Interest on a Loan

++++++++++++++++++++++++++++++++

There are all sorts of reasons people take out loans—to pay for school, to start a business, to renovate a home, and more—but keep in mind that you aren't just repaying the principal. You must also repay interest. In this activity, we'll use simple interest to estimate how much you would need to pay back on a loan. But keep in mind that in the real world, there are a lot of factors that can complicate these calculations. If you'd like to learn more, there are online calculators that you can use to create different scenarios. For instance, if the interest compounds, you'll need to pay a lot more! This is why you may have heard adults complaining about student loans.

1. a. How much interest will you have to pay on a loan of $2,000 at 4% interest for three years?

    $2,000 x 4% x 3 = $ __240__

    b. What is the total amount you will have to pay back on this loan?

    $2,000 + $ __240__ = $__2,240__

2. a. How much interest will you pay on a loan of $300 at 12.3% interest for two years?

    $300 x 12.3% x 2 = $73.80

    b. What is the total amount you will have to pay back on this loan?

    $300 + $__73.80__=$__373.80__

3. a. How much interest will you pay on a loan of $700 at 6.3% interest for five years?

    $700 x 6.3% x 5 = $220.50

    b. What is the total amount you will have to pay back on this loan?

    $700 + $__220.50__=$__920.50__

4. a. How much interest will you pay on a loan of $2,000 at 5.5% interest for seven years?

    $2,000 x 5.5% x 7 = $770

    b. What is the total amount you will have to pay back on this loan?

    $2,000 + $770 =$2,770

5. a. How much interest will you pay on a loan of $1,500 at 5% interest for three years?

    $1,500 x 5% x 3 = $225

    b. What is the total amount you will have to pay back on this loan?

    $1,500 + $225 =$1,725

6. a. How much interest will you pay on a loan of $24,000 at 7% interest for five years?

    $24,000 x 7% x 5 = $8,400

    b. What is the total amount you will have to pay back on this loan?

    $24,000 + $8,400 =$32,400

7. a. How much interest will you pay on a loan of $25,500 at 2.75% interest for sixteen years?

    $25,500 x 2.75% x 16 = $11,220

    b. What is the total amount you will have to pay back on this loan?

    $25,500 + $11,220 =$36,720

45 Calculating Credit Interest

++++++++++++++++++++++++++++++++

Credit cards have an APR, or annual percentage rate, that is applied to any outstanding money you owe after each billing period. If you want to calculate how much interest your balance accrues in a month, you divide the APR by 12 and multiply it against your balance. Let's practice calculating interest.

1. Izzie uses her credit card to buy airplane tickets in May. Her credit card payment is due at the end of June. She does not pay her full balance and carries over $500. If her APR is 12%, then how much interest will she accrue for the month of July?

    $500 x (12% ÷ 12) = $500 x 1%

    = $500 x 0.01 = $5

2. Mima moves into a new apartment and spends $2,000 on things for her new home in October. Her payment is due at the end of November, but she pays only $1,000. If her APR is 12%, how much interest will she accrue by the end of December?

    ($2,000 − $1,000) x (12% ÷ 12) = $1,000 x 1%

    = $1,000 x 0.01 = $10

3. Gordon buys a new bicycle for $210. He makes the minimum monthly payment of $20. How much interest will he accrue in the first month, if his APR is 12%?

    ($210 − $20) x (12% ÷ 12) = $190 x 1%

    = $190 x 0.01 = $1.90

4. Xavier spends $1,335 and pays the minimum payment of $35. How much interest will he accrue in the first month, if his APR is 6%?

    ($1,335 − $35) x (6% ÷ 12) = $1,300 x 0.5%

    = $1,300 x 0.005 = $6.50